THE ART OF
HAPPINESS

John Cowper Powys

SIMON AND SCHUSTER
New York · 1935

Dedicated

to

MR. AND MRS. A. G. AND A. S. KRICK

My Nearest Neighbors

in

Columbia County

TABLE OF CONTENTS

THE ART OF
HAPPINESS

THE ROOT OF THE MATTER

Happiness is not a by-product—This book's basic axiom—The mind's control of its own thoughts—The necessity for faith—Happiness distinguished from pleasure—Passive and active happiness—Why is there no cult of happiness?—Happiness not a product of political life—Our Egoism—The Ichthian leap—The act of De-carnation—How to think of death—What to do when life-weary—Misery, Apathy, Worry.

ANY DISCUSSION ABOUT WHAT IS THE PURPOSE OF life, or about what is the good life, or about what is the ideal life, carries a rather hollow sound in these reckless and cynical times; but, after all, such questions *are* being dealt with, at least in minor issues, by the individual conscience every day; and if a writer has the gall to bring up this ancient problem, and the wit to apply it to modern conditions, I cannot see that he is beating the air. No amount of cynicism seems to save our individual conscience from distressing struggles; and in these struggles, whatever our philosophy may be, the value we place on Happiness and the meaning we attach to Happiness must play a part.

— 3 —

Happiness differs from Pleasure in this very thing, namely that the idea of *quality,* the idea of something mental and emotional, of something intellectual and what used to be called "spiritual," is added, in it, to the more sensual feeling. A man could be happy while he was in the act of sacrificing his life, whereas we should scruple about using the word pleasure in this connection.

I must confess it is hard for me to see how what we call Happiness (and I think the word has come to mean that particular glow of well-being that arises when something deep in us is being satisfied and fulfilled) can take any place but the highest place in our estimate of life's highest good.

Try to substitute any other *summum bonum* for this one, and you will see how many difficulties you get into! What religious person for instance would make the aim of life the process of knowing God, and becoming one with God, if this conscious harmony with the spirit underlying the system of things did not imply personal happiness?

And it would seem a weird and unnatural thing for a man to pursue what is called "Truth," either by strictly scientific, or by the more imaginative philosophical method, if this pursuit were not in itself attended by happiness or at least presumed to result in happiness. And the same thing applies to that mysterious relation, between what is half-created by the mind and what is half-discovered in nature, which we call Beauty. If artists and poets and story-tellers didn't find, and their audiences find, happiness in this particular human activity, it would surely never have become the mighty urge that it has become.

And what applies to Truth and Beauty applies to what we have come to call Goodness too. If to be good didn't mean both to be happy and to be a cause of happiness, there surely could never have arisen in the world this great "stream of tendency making for righteousness" such as we cannot help—for all our reversions to barbarity—being aware of in ourselves and in history.

And the same thing holds in the matter of practical work. It is all very well for Carlyle to harp upon work, as against happiness, as the purpose of life. But we are men; we are not machines. It is not work *in itself,* any more than it is God in Himself, or truth in itself, or beauty in itself, that keeps us going. It is the happiness that we get from work, or give by work, either immediately or in the long run, that drives us forward.

There does seem to be a wide-spread notion, however, that although in reality all these great "purposes" of life, God, Truth, Beauty, Goodness, Work, are precious to us because they alone, in the long run, bring us happiness, we can only obtain this happiness, or create this happiness, by treating these things *as ends in themselves* and by letting the happiness they bring, their *by-product,* come and go as it will.

But is not this attitude of mind, when you really analyse it, a pathological superstition? Does not its prevalence prove, not the sacredness of God, Truth, Beauty, Goodness, Work, but the sacredness of the feeling of happiness, a feeling so precious, so rare, so sacred in fact that we all are secretly afraid—as the ancients were in regard to those Avenging Deities that they called the Eumenides—to so much as name in our hearts what we know to be the feeling that really keeps us going and keeps the world going?

This work is therefore an experiment, an experiment for both writer and reader, to see what effect it has upon the mind if we habitually destroy this happiness-taboo, and aim at building up for ourselves—and incidentally for others—a premeditated system or art of personal happiness out of the various orderly and disorderly elements that the fatality of our character and the accidents of our environment and our experience offer as our destined and chance-given material.

The only axiom I must beg the reader to accept at the start—even if he be rationally committed to some system of fatalism or determinism — is the basic axiom that our thoughts at least are more or less under our control.

This is really the root of the matter. If you refuse to allow that the human mind has any control over its thoughts I cannot see what good you can possibly get—except the satisfaction of studying a fellow-dupe's illusions—from a book of this kind. It must appear to you mere pretentious gabble. But if you grant this one single axiom, that the mind has at least a partial control over its thoughts, I think I can deduce, though with no exact or mathematical inevitableness, but still with a measure of convincingness, a good many important conclusions.

Granting, first of all, then, that the mind *has* some control over its thoughts, let us for a moment examine the nature of this control.

What do we mean by the controlling "mind," and what do we mean by the controlled "thoughts"?

At this point it is necessary—in spite of the technical objections that professional psychologists will raise—to use the old simple natural human words for those natural, if not simple, movements of the mind, feelings of the ego, and conscious sensations of the inner self which accompany all mental acts.

The "mind" is *the self when it thinks to itself;* and its "thoughts" are *what it thinks.* The self, as a mind thinking, has the power of detaching itself from all its bodily feelings and sensations. It can even detach itself from its consciousness of itself as a mind with certain particular thoughts. I mean that it can—and I think this is a universal human experience—stand, so to speak, *beside itself,* and say to itself, "That is you, you old Identity, thinking the same troublesome worrying thoughts as usual!"

The more we consider this matter of the mind's control — of even its partial control — over its thoughts, the more we are compelled to recognise that these thoughts are intimately associated with the fact of our being happy or unhappy. Thoughts have the power of making us feel happy even while our body is suffering; and as we all know they very often have the power of making us profoundly unhappy when our body is completely at ease and even enjoying pleasant sensations.

My own mind dwells so constantly on the verge of certain terrible manias that it can speak with peculiar authority upon a pathological subject like this.

What I want to make clear is simple enough. When we talk of "the mind controlling its thoughts" what we are especially thinking of is the mind's power of making us feel happy by calling up certain thoughts while it dismisses certain other thoughts.

Most of us, I suppose, even if we are what are called "healthy-minded," have some peculiar dreads, apprehensions, fears, loathings, horrors, to dwell upon which is extremely painful to us and to forget which is a heavenly relief. I doubt whether we can prevent these thoughts' first appearances, but the mind has the power of either dwelling on them or of forcing itself to forget them; and what I myself have discovered, from examining the behaviour of my own mind, is that there is a cruel demon hidden in it that derives sadistic pleasure from trying to force me to think of the very things that especially make me shudder. And the happier I feel, and the pleasanter, in other respects, the moment is, the more energetically does this demon under my own helmet call to my attention what I particularly loathe to think about.

Whether there is such a thing as a "faculty" of the mind exactly corresponding to what we popularly mean by the word "will" does not affect what I am saying. It is fashionable now-a-days to dislike the idea of "faculties of the mind" and it is also fashionable now-a-days especially to dislike the notion of a mental activity called "the use of the will"; but it surely remains that there is some movement of our deepest self, some psychic experience common to us, which, whether you call it by the word "will" or by some other name, is an important aspect of all human psychology.

What I mean is that there is something in the actual working of our minds, which, if you are too pedantic to call it by the popular monosyllable "will," you will have to designate by *some* word when you wish to express a universal subjective feeling that we all have whether it be an illusion or not.

But at this point it is necessary for me to use a word still more unfashionable than the word "will" and with even a worse odour of archaic superstition —I refer to the word "faith." For as a matter of fact what you really experience in your mind is the power of transmitting a positive or a negative vibration to yourself in regard to your thoughts; selecting, rejecting, encouraging, dismissing, suppressing, as your mood decides.

It is to this decisive motion within your consciousness that the use-and-wont of popular speech gives the name "will"; and when you transmit this order to think further, or *not* to think further, along a particular line, or to summon up, or *not* to summon up a particular image, you are doing what is usually called—and we must give *some* name to this familiar process—"using your will."

And it is just here, it seems to me, that it is legitimate to use the word "faith." What you have, in fact, before you make this motion of your will, is the faith that it will prove effective; and that the "thought" in question, which may well have come into your head without your volition, will obey your command, and either remain and emphasize itself or vanish away.

Supposing that you have got into the habit of indulging in a fatalistic way of feeling about the mystery of consciousness this "faith" in your power over your thoughts may be extremely weak, and though you may feebly transmit your command and say to yourself, "But I won't think any more about *that!*" there is no formidable battery of faith, behind the vibration you transmit to give you assurance that your interference with your thoughts will be obeyed. It is for this reason that I have come to feel—and my feeling has been justified by repeated subjective experiences—that at the root of the whole matter lies what you might call *the necessity for faith,* for faith in your power to regulate your own thoughts, for faith in the power of your subjective will.

We have reached the point then of being in a position—granting the validity of this faith in our power to select between our thoughts—to maintain the proposition that it lies in our power to encourage the thoughts that bring us happiness and to suppress the others.

But what kind of thing is this "happiness" we are considering? That is the next matter to be discussed. We all know roughly what the words Happiness and Unhappiness mean, but like all human names for important reactions to life they seem to indicate states of feeling that quickly tend to blend with, and lose themselves in, other states of feeling, for which there have been found, by the selective instinct of our particular tribe, quite different names.

Joy, ecstasy, rapture, delight, satisfaction, enchantment, peace, contentment, enjoyment, blessedness, pleasure—all these indicate conditions of human feeling that cannot be rigidly separated off from what we call Happiness. Pleasure, I suppose comes on the whole nearest to it in our ordinary speech and the antithesis Pleasure—Pain corresponds roughly, in most of our minds, with the antithesis Happiness —Unhappiness.

Pain, however, though applicable as we all know to mental suffering, strictly belongs to the physical side of things, while even *Pleasure,* the other member of this great rival antithesis, though less consistently than *Pain,* has like it a physical implication.

There is always a considerable margin, a sort of obscure twilight-nimbus, left vague and undetermined around every great human word, as it descends the stream of the generations, and certain important nuances of meaning are constantly being added, while others are being taken away, without the possibility of any individual mind in one life-time catching the drift of the change.

Personally I like the sound of the word "pleasure" a good deal better than the sound of the word "happiness." There seems to me something at once more fluid and more organic about it; while the word "pain" is certainly more expressive than the word "unhappiness." The syllables "happy" have something jaunty about them, something brisk and bouncing. They suggest an element less dignified, less poetical, than the psychic over-tone conveyed in the syllables "pleasure." Take for instance that characteristic line of Wordsworth's, "The pleasure which there is in life itself," and substitute the word "happiness." It would not be only the scansion of the verse that would be broken. There would be a loss of some deep organic quality in the meaning.

Nevertheless, in spite of the annoying jauntiness, and even the bouncing babyishness, of the word "happy," it is hard to see how it can be avoided. What it possesses, that the more poetical word "pleasure" lacks, is an over-tone of mental volition. You can will to be happy—you cannot evoke the mystery of pleasure by any willing.

It seems indeed as though happiness might be considered the subjective counterpart to pleasure. I mean that while it would be natural to say: "Be happy or die!" there would be something strained, something even violent, about the expression: "Get pleasure or die!" The more you concentrate on the difference between these words the more clearly does it appear that while pleasure is something that comes to you from outside, happiness is something that, though it may often be "roused to reciprocity" by pleasure, is intrinsically a mental, or even a moral state. You could also, I think, maintain without contradiction that there is an implication of lastingness about happiness, whereas the idea of pleasure suggests something not only more physical but much more transitory.

Having thus dealt with the meaning of our word I want now to dig down if I can to the basic root-psychology of the feeling, or sensation, or emotion which the word conveys.

I think we find, as with most things in the world, an unmistakable duality in the nature of happiness itself, quite irrespective of its basic opposition to its antagonist in the happy-unhappy antithesis. The thing can be a passive state or it can be an active state. At its best in its passive condition it gives you the feeling of a certain lying back in delicious receptivity upon the life-stream whose waves rock you and whose flood bears you up.

At its best in its active state it gives you the feeling of a vibrant energy, of a strong, tense self-creation, a feeling full of the glow of battle and of the exultation of wrestling with a formidable opponent.

Now since there exists this basic difference between the passive feeling of happiness, when a person lies back upon life, and the active feeling, when he wrestles with life, the crucial question arises, upon which of these two moods—granting, as in practical life we have to grant, that what we call our "will" represents a vital mental process in our living organism—it is better to concentrate. I mean if we do really have power over our thought-processes, is it wiser to aim at the active state of happiness, or at the passive? I would say most strongly in answer to this that the wise course is to aim for both. Nor can they altogether be separated; for both require *some* measure of deliberate effort. The tense, the strung-up, the creative side of the feeling of happiness is not completely absent, at least at the start, from the other mood. For the yielded, passive, relaxed, abandoned state, though it does fall to the lot of certain people to enjoy it by pure good luck, can be made much more continuous by intensifying what we may possess of the tense, alert, self-conscious, and "gathered-up," attitude.

We are all familiar with the expression, "Pull yourself together." Well! that expression, better than any other, describes the psychological movement by which in our deepest soul we put on, as Homer would say, "our harness," and wrestle with the world.

But the point is that the relaxed and passive kind of happiness, when you float on the ocean of the exterior cosmos and allow its magical currents to flow through you, is a kind of happiness that can be reached deliberately and enjoyed deliberately when once you have acquired the trick of "pulling yourself together."

Such magical, abandoned moods *do* come—it would be absurd to deny it—to the most casual, the most natural, the most unconscious people; but they come to the conscious, philosophical ones—it is certainly safe to say *that* much—in proportion as these latter clear the way the more intensely and the more craftily for their reception.

The truth is that when once we have arrived, as so many of us have, at a point where we cannot escape being conscious of every flicker of our sensuous and mental life, it is ridiculous to tell us to be natural and simple and unaffected without allowing us the right, or even the possibility, of consciously struggling after this simplicity, this naturalness, this unaffectedness. The clue to the whole life-history of the human mind from the beginning until this day lies in those three-fold spiral curves, so beautifully indicated by Hegel, wherein we begin with the religious simplicity of children, advance to the cynical rationalism of youth, and then return—only with a difference—to the old childish wonder, in our mellowest and most inspired maturity.

But, granting that we have a right to make a cult of personal happiness and to make as simple a cult and as childish a cult of it as we please, the point arises, how is it that among all the other ideals put forward at the great historic epochs of the world for the human race to follow, the cult of personal happiness hardly appears at all?

What are the reasons why so few human beings dare deliberately, even to themselves, make their personal happiness the main purpose of their lives? Is it all due to that curious taboo on the matter about which I have already spoken? I think another cause of it is that there is a great evolutional pressure focussed just now upon the human race. The lower animals have slipped aside from this terrible pressure. They have stereotyped themselves into a happy stagnation; and even the plants, save when meddled with by man, have fallen into the peaceful recurrence of what is outside *the fearful intention* of evolution.

But luckless man—made to be a pot for the creative fire by the mysterious master-force—feels driving, burning, scorching, fermenting, seething through him the same dreadful urge to self-lacerating progress which at the beginning forced our ancestors out of their sprawlings and stretchings and baskings into the tyranny of mind.

It is, I think, this terrific evolutionary pressure

springing out of the power behind nature, rather than any superstitious guilt-sense derived from the sin-rituals of savage antiquity, that mainly accounts for the fact that among all our historic moral systems there is no widespread or profoundly influential cult advocating personal happiness as the chief purpose of human life. The Epicurean philosophy itself was, it seems in reality, not *quite* this; and as for the doctrines of Aristippus, which do seem to have amounted to this, they can have been scarcely known beyond an Athenian circle of progressive minds and beyond the ardent youth of a few Ionian islands.

In China no doubt, in Arabia Felix and in Persia, such a theory found its advocates, but I question whether among the metaphysical intellects of India it ever gained much hearing.

The modern Western tendency, both among Communists and Fascists, is so furiously social that all types of individualistic thought are under a ban, tarred with the invidious brush of bourgeois liberalism.

And yet when you come down to brass tacks there surely must arise, every day of their devoted lives, in these young people—for these violent Western ideals seem especially to answer the needs of generous youth—moments when they feel that in this one single terrestrial experience of a living soul, "between two eternities," it is a queer thing to be thinking of nothing but the material well-being of future generations.

What I am trying to suggest here is that a stoical resolve to endure life happily, without abating a jot of the gathering-up of the resources of our spirit, is not an unworthy human ideal.

Why should the integration, the self-realisation of our human ego, the gathering together in a deliberate tension of our life-forces, be, for a whole epoch of human history, so entirely absorbed in external activity that the inner life of the individual, his sensuous and mystical response to life, is reduced to the minimum?

Surely a person can be an honourable citizen of his country and yet feel that the one thing needful, since after all he *is* a personal ego and not just a cog in a machine or an ant in an ant-heap, is to enrich and simplify his own private response to the universe.

It was faith in a personal religion that so often gave our ancestors the spirit to endure life with stoical calm and enjoy life with unflinching zest. *Their* ideal was an individual life and to this they adapted themselves by the stately practise of their old-fashioned mental and spiritual "yoga," a "yoga" that after all possessed its own imaginative stir and its own psychological excitement.

I cannot see why the devotion to a communistic

or fascist state, any more than a devotion to business or games, should be allowed to absorb all our superfluous energy—that *marginal energy of mankind* the disposal of which is so intimate a problem—or to exploit to social purpose minds that are made for a response to the cosmos.

In throwing overboard the old-fashioned religious life, which, after all, held the clue to deep psychological responses to the universe, we have permitted political and social idealism to usurp a place in the life of our solitary soul for which they are entirely unfitted; with the result that since these aggressive invaders cannot fill up these spacious rooms, nor feel comfortable in these stately presence-chambers, there are forlorn spaces left, spaces completely untenanted through which unhappy phantoms stalk and maniac-abortions gibber.

The human soul has a long history. It carries about it high mysterious memories, that like nightwinds fluttering the faded arras of an ancestral chamber throw into momentary relief dim motions of forgotten figures whose terrible beauty once transformed our life. No human soul is really satisfied through all of its being by an existence devoted to what is called the "Service of Humanity," still less by the Service of the State. It demands more than these things; and to bind it down to these things is to prepare for terrible and insane reversions to lost idolatries.

Driven as we are by the urge of economic necessity, hemmed in as we are by the fatality of our material environment, there is a margin in all our lives when, whether we like it or not, our thoughts and emotions wander from the matter in hand, and our imagination finds itself confronted by mysteries beyond the improvement of any human society.

Futile as it may be to fancy we can discover in life, or invent for life, any universal "purpose" or underlying "meaning," there yet remains something in us—call it by what name you will—that relucts at subsiding into the rôle of patient labourers for the good of posterity. Eliminate all superstition, all "other-worldliness," all sense of "sin," be as sceptical as you please about God and Immortality, there still exists, in the most regimented and docile ego, an intellectual restlessness, a stirring of the imagination, a troubling of the waters, a terrible and dangerous questioning, that cannot be allayed by any national or even by any international pre-occupation.

The soul within us is a microcosm, not a micropolis; and is born for the happiness that flows from a cosmic, not a political or economic life. There is a craving in us, felt by men and women of every colour and every race, that neither the passion for communal improvement nor the passion for communal applause can distract from its organic unrest.

We are men; and it is the destiny of men to detach themselves from the universe in order to enjoy the universe. Action, however exciting, labour, however absorbing, penury, however exacting, love and hate, however obsessing, leave a yawning gap in the circumference of our life. You may beat this exigency down; you may starve it out; you may crowd it away; the thing refuses to be altogether killed! A devoted existence is not enough. Virtue is not enough. Heroic self-sacrifice is not enough. The soul of man can only be fed at the breasts of the universal.

And this remains true even if, as some insist, we reduce the "soul" to a mere name for the unifying vital principle of our bodily organism.

Personally, like Malvolio, I think highly of the soul; but if it were no more than the focus-point of our magnetic energy, it would still refuse to content itself with mere work and mere play.

Against all our instincts for comfort and security this trouble in the soul stirs us up and drives us on, to "gather our forces together" and wrestle with the mystery of life and death. I think it is partly because of this spiritual restlessness in us that the idea of the pursuit of personal happiness as an adequate "purpose of life" strikes us as uninspiring and unworthy. As a matter of fact it ceases to be uninspiring and unworthy when we concentrate on the *quality* of the happiness we seek. No one would dare to call the happiness of a lover, of a saint, of an artist, of a mystic, uninspiring. Indeed in regard to the quality of the happiness we are discussing I come bolt up against the real crux of the whole matter. The soul remains as much unsatisfied by a life of ordinary labour as it does by a life of heroic devotion to some communal cause. It demands, and it has a right to demand, deep draughts of a particular kind of magical happiness such as do not necessarily follow from any self-sacrifice.

It demands a happiness flowing into it straight from the elements, straight from the universe, straight from the basic mystery of life and death. If you are not able to force yourself to feel this sort of thing for some moments of time every day of your life you are being defrauded of your birthright as an offspring of the cosmos. None but a madman would deny that extreme cold, extreme hunger, extreme pain, are things that can bring down all but the sublimest characters. So also, if you care greatly for another living person, that person's prostration under these extreme evils will probably break you down.

But the point is that there always remains the hope that these intolerable evils will pass. Many and many a suicide would be alive still if he could only have waited till some particular accumulation of evils had passed, as everything does pass in the casuality of time.

But even if there were more unbearable pain in the world than there is, *that* were no reason for rejecting these magical sensations or for refusing to struggle after them.

The evolutionary force in the universe having once issued in personality, nothing short of such moods, such attitudes, such exultations in our personal life is worthy of our cosmic origin.

It is indeed likely enough, in spite of the modern tendency to lay all the stress upon the material world, that the highest part of our personality is already in touch, *is already part of,* a higher dimension of life than is supplied by the phenomena of the astronomical universe.

Metaphysicians tend to speak of this higher level of our identity as something impersonal; but they are just as likely to be wrong as to be right in this misanthropic assertion. It may well be, on the contrary, that this "higher," or "deeper," or more "comprehensive" aspect of our ego is the most intensely personal thing about us! The sublime and startling dogma of the Catholic Church in the matter of the Incarnation *may* be representative of a tremendous cosmic secret.

But whether this is so or not, whether there be or not a level of life outside the phenomenal world to which the apex, so to speak, of our living organism pierces its way, what I want to insist upon now is that the effort we make to gather our forces together "to be happy or die" is an effort not only able to satisfy that restless soul within us which remains unsatisfied by benevolence and righteousness, but is an effort that automatically forces our nature into unity with itself, bringing our senses into relation with our intellect, and both of these into relation with that mysterious apex of our personality that loses itself in the unknown.

My own experience is that Heraclitus was right when he said, *"Life is War";* but this experience does not preclude that in the nobler human society of this future such war will be purely between the soul and the universe. I only mean that I have discovered that by the use of a certain strain and a certain tension, as if you were engaged in a struggle against a powerful antagonist, it is possible to force the senses to respond to the magic of the elements at the same moment as you force the intellect into an awareness of our cosmic predicament.

And thus I come to what is really the root-matter in this ticklish discussion. Since the evolutionary pressure in the universe, working through the vital instincts of living organisms, has produced, as the most complicated result we are as yet certain of, the conscious intelligences of individual men and women, and since it seems as though at the present moment the driving force of this evolutionary pressure, its apex-point of advance, *is through the human intelligence,* it surely becomes probable that whatever "the purpose of life" may be from an ultimate cosmic viewpoint, as far as we are concerned it has to do with personality and with the nature and quality of personal life.

What is popularly known as "Egoism" is therefore a mental attitude, not only lawful, but inescapable and inevitable, if we are to be in harmony with the main pressure of the cosmic tide; whereas what is popularly known as "egotism," or in plainer speech "selfishness," is simply the abuse of egoism, or egoism exerting itself in an unintelligent, clumsy, and insensitive way.

But we can go much further in this distinction between the commendable instinct we call egoism and its abuse in selfishness.

Although the cosmic purpose, relative to our human intelligence, seems now to be concerned with the development of personality, man remains historically and practically a creature dependent on others, nourished by others, attracted and repelled by others, and under the dominance of the economic customs of the place of his birth.

The arena of our struggle is therefore complicated for most of us by being composed of not only natural elements but of very touchy and very jumpy human beings.

Interrupting the direct contact of our individual soul with the cosmos, we have to cope with a number of neighbour-souls who are also struggling to realise their identities under the impact of our common environment.

It is in the blending of our relations with our neighbors and with the universe, or, to use the old language, with "Man" and with "God," that the quality of our egoism becomes apparent. You can have the egoism of a sea-gull or the egoism of a hedgehog and be justified in both; whereas there is a certain kind of selfishness that leaves your personality withered, colourless, sapless and neutral, just as there is a certain kind of unselfishness that produces these disagreeable effects. To be a supremely successful egoist it is necessary to combine a devilish cunning with a sublime unscrupulousness and both these things with the detachment of a saint, but fortunately Nature is more merciful as well as more cruel than most philosophers upon happiness realise, and without aspiring to attain this extreme mixture of Machiavellism and Spinozism a person may pick up a good number of windfalls of the most subtle happiness every day of his life if he will follow a few of the ancient ritual-tricks, in this art, that I am now fumbling to express.

I have called this first chapter "The Root of the Matter" and I want to reveal now, without more ado, what I have found in my own experience to be the best ritual-trick or habitual motion of the mind, wherewith not only to bear up against the pressure of external evils, or against that "whoreson lethargy" in a person's soul which comes both from mental weariness and bodily weakness, but actually, though the sense of it may be faint, to rouse in the heart the spring of happiness.

I shall enlarge later on this subject, but it must suffice now to indicate in general terms what I have in my head. It has to do with a motion of the mind that I call the *Ichthian act* because it bears a remote resemblance to the leap of a fish out of the water, into the air, and back again into the water.

The cause of so many vague feelings of unhappiness, apart from acute physical distress, is almost always the pressure upon us of some mental worry, or nervous depression, or what one might describe as "the illusion of the commonplace."

The great thing is to take our cue from Heraclitus and regard the gloomy moment as a challenge to our spirit, a challenge to close with the invisible enemy in a life-and-death struggle.

Shake off the pessimistic assumption that to be unhappy is inevitable. To encounter such evil and oppressive moments is certainly inevitable. But it is no cause for crying, "Just like my luck!" or for sighing, "Pity poor me again!" It is the fortune of war. It is one of the terms on which we wrestle with this chaotic world.

What I mean by the "Ichthian act" is a swift lumping together of all the evils of your life—as if you turned them into one element that completely surrounds you—followed by a fierce leap up of your inmost identity, a leap that takes you, if only for a second, into the freer air.

In this second you plunge through, and leap out of, the lumped-together evil of life, not in the strength of any outward change of conditions, or of any hope of such a change, but solely in a spasmodic revolt against them, a revolt wherein the indestructible spirit at the bottom of your soul refuses to yield.

I have taken the expression "Ichthian" from the Greek word "Ichthus" because of its Early Christian use, meaning Christ the Saviour. In this case the "Saviour" is our own spirit of ultimate defiance; but so seldom do we draw upon this spirit in us that, when we do, it seems like the aid of a supernatural presence.

There come moments, however, when this self-evoked leap of resistance is impossible for us because of our weakness and our melancholy; and for such occasions, while I am touching upon this "Root of the Matter," I want to hint at a different and less violent spiritual procedure. For this also I have a presumptuous and arbitrary name—I call it the act of "De-carnation." Just as by Incarnation we mean the mystic fusion of the spirit with the flesh, so by "de-carnation" I mean the separation of the spirit in us *from* our flesh.

The act of de-carnation is a much easier one than what I call the "Ichthian" act. It consists in thinking of your soul as something separate from your body, something that exists in the air—that free air into which the Ichthian leap carries your whole identity —by the side of your oppressed and persecuted body.

Within this soul, thus separated from your body —and the play of imagination required for this mental act is an old and very simple one, known in some degree to us all—dwells now the main part of your consciousness; and from this vantage-point it surveys and overlooks your persecuted and weighed-down body.

In no circumstance does this act of de-carnation help you more completely than when, confronted by some other person who is being a trial to you, you are tempted to pit your egoism, your desire for happiness at his or her expense, against the similar desire in this trying person. But when, hovering in the free air apart from both the self-asserting ones, you envisage yourself and this other as if you were a third person at the encounter, you are in a position to experience an extraordinary liberation of spirit and a curiously indulgent attitude, both towards the troublesome intruder on your peace and towards your own agitated and egoistic organism. You are aloof from both and, as it were, watching both from your airy vantage-ground. Your soul is still *the centre of your awareness,* but no longer the centre of your touchy animal identity.

As contrasted with this temporary de-carnation what I am trying to indicate by what I call the Ichthian act is a resolute motion of subjective energy within the ego by means of which our spirit rises up from the depths of our being and shaking off both physical lethargy and mental discomfort plunges into the mystery of life, considered as one great stream, and into the mystery of death, considered as a positive element surrounding it.

In either case the soul's existence, as Heraclitus says, is a state of war, war down to the roots of things; but you can either fight this abysmal battle by the act of aloofness which I have indicated in the word de-carnation, or by the act of intense integration to which I have given the name Ichthian.

The truth is we submit far too much and far too humbly to the pressure of the daily miseries implied in our ordinary life. When not ourselves in extreme pain, when not sharing by the sympathy of our nerves the extreme pain of another, who is there shall dare to put limits to what the human mind, fortified by a practised will, can achieve in the evoking of happiness and peace?

We stand indeed between two extremes. On the one hand we can pursue what is popularly called "pleasure," grossly, heedlessly, selfishly, at the expense of all finer considerations. On the other hand we can let our personal life go and give ourselves up to some absorbing Cause which becomes more to us than soul or body.

Neither of these is the way suggested in this book; for the clutching at external pleasure puts the spirit within us and the happiness within us at the mercy of accident, while the heroic sacrificing of our personal life on the altar of a cause that may or may not benefit future generations leaves the great evolutionary tide that has culminated in our life, thwarted, perverted, dissipated, squandered, offered up to a future that after all may never be moulded according to our ideal.

In laying stress upon the gathering together of the forces of the soul in this fish-like leap of primordial desperation I feel I am describing an universal psychological experience. Where it is not recognised as such, I would say that the person in question is in some way sub-normal, sub-vital, sub-magnetic.

I call it "the Ichthian act" because I want to suggest by the analogy of the fish leaping into the air out of the water an act of the soul that is the most comprehensive act the soul can make, an act that includes not only an embrace of the mystery of life, but an embrace of the mystery of death, considered as something positive. The Ichthus or fish, swimming in the water, is like our soul in its practical absorption in the diurnal routine of its existence; but when it leaps into the air, to fall back again with that familiar sound which is one of the most poetical sounds in nature, it leaves for the moment its proper element and invades a super-element, an element which might well be compared with the *other-dimensional* mystery which surrounds our mortal existence. The leaping fish does in fact—for the air into which it leaps would be its death if it couldn't sink back into water—represent the soul embracing both life and death in a moment of predetermined intensity. Montaigne seems to imply that all wise men meditate on the *nothingness* of death and thus escape the fear of it. Goethe seems anxious on the contrary to have us put the thought of death completely out of our minds. Neither of these methods of dealing with this circumference of our life seems to me satisfactory. Montaigne's brooding on it and reiterated self-reassurings about it come at last to resemble the uneasy fidgettings of a life-worshipper confronted with his grand antagonist, whereas Goethe's habitual way of shying off the whole subject, as, for instance, in that "Think of Living" written over Mignon's tomb, seems no more than a child-like turning from the dark.

The best way to take death as far as I can see, is not to avoid all thought of it, though there is more to be said for that method than for brooding on its annihilating negations, but to think of it in some *positive* way, as possessing, equally with life, some tremendous withheld secret.

This way of thinking of it need not be very distinct—it obviously cannot be, where we are in such absolute ignorance—but it *can* be positive and it can be hopeful. We have an equal right, as far as the "Truth" of this dark matter goes, to be hopeful as to be despairing, for our ignorance is complete; but since there is really a half-chance that the mind's attitude counts for something—I mean that a life-long concentration on the idea of surviving death might be an element in our surviving it—it does not seem the part of wisdom to brood obstinately and dogmatically upon annihilation; unless annihilation, as may easily happen, *is what you want.*

The wisest course it seems to me, since no one can deny that both these issues, survival and annihilation, are equally possible, is to combine them in some vague way, and formulate in your mind an imaginative conception of death, or even an imaginative image of death, that shall allow for the feeling of annihilation, of *something* annihilated, as well as for the feeling of survival, of *something* surviving.

This cannot be so very hard to do, since both annihilation and survival are matters of daily experience in regard to other things than ourselves. Each of my abysmal motions of the soul when it finds itself "up against it," this Ichthian act and this de-carnating act, have something in them of both living and dying.

When certain vigorous people die—and our best tragic actors are aware of this—there is a spasm, a convulsion, a magnetic shock, a shudder, like that of a tense-drawn bow-string let go; and although my Ichthian act by which we plunge into a life-and-death exultation is not so spasmodic or so convulsed as this, there is the same "inbreathing" and "outbreathing," the same pressing down of a spring, the same releasing of a spring, the same plunge from element into element, the same intensification of identity and dispersing of identity.

And just as this particular human gesture—so general as to be practically universal—has something in common with a fish's leap into the air, so it has something in common with culmination of the erotic act. There is the same complete shaking off of all ordinary pre-occupation, the same complete abandonment to a super-sensation, the same half-creation and half-discovery of a cosmic focus-point.

It does not need any catastrophic calamity, any overwhelming tragedy, to drive us poor mortals to desperation. You have to be an unusually well-constituted person to be able to get through a single day of human life without a threat upon your peace by some kind of devilish misery. It is at these moments that the test comes as to whether our philosophy is worth its salt or not.

Well! There you are, a conscious human soul in a tired and distressed body, menaced by some sort of horrid darkening of the lamp of your vital spirit of resistance; and what are you going to do? You can, of course, get through it—we generally do *somehow* —with a lamentable sigh, or a doleful curse, or with bitter tears; but the point I want to make now is that it is possible by a mental movement that in time becomes automatic, to defeat and drive back this mood of misery, and even attain, under the very horns and stench of this palpable devil, a tolerable modicum of defiant happiness.

My own procedure under these conditions is to try the Ichthian plunge first, if I have energy enough; but, if not, to fling myself into the aloofness of the de-carnation trick. Force your soul to leap up from the depths of your being. Force it to make of the material pressure round you a typical specimen of the hardness and prickliness and scaliness and dreariness of the devilish side of life.

Lump the evils together, the physical ones, the mental ones, and the whole damned outfit. Then, pulling *yourself* together, wrestle with the accumulated mass, selecting out of it one or two of its more tolerable aspects upon which you can concentrate without especial loathing; or, if there are no redeeming features in it at all, concentrating on the chemical constituents of your cul-de-sac, on the elements of air and water and earth and fire, which must in *some* form be present, if only in the shape of dirty boards, darkened stones, misty windows, and a dripping faucet.

Don't, whatever you do, begin to pity yourself; still less begin to curse your fate or the day of your birth. Avoid, like the devil, any comparison between your luck and other people's luck. Say to yourself, "This is life and I am a child of life; and what I've got to do is to wrestle with this loathsome-lovely mother of mine as long as I've got any breath in my body and any consciousness in my mind!"

But not content with wrestling in this desperate way with life and crying out to it, "Thou *shalt* bless me! Thou *shalt* bless me!" as you force some wretched simulacra of the planetary elements to supply the place of earth and sky and air and sea, it is a good trick to think of the whole innumerable company of the dead that these elements have gendered and have swallowed up; and to think of the round earth, floating in space, as bulging and brimming with death, just as it is heaving and quivering with life.

Thinking so, as your soul struggles with the evil of that moment, there is no force in the world that can prevent your recognition that there is some mystery behind it all; and that this planetary world spawning life and filling up mortuaries and ossuaries of death is only one dimension of the unfathomable secret of what is.

All minor miseries have a viaduct, a drain, a channel, a canal, a culvert, running into the bottomless lake of universal death; and down this channel it is good to travel as often as we may! If we imagined ourselves dead more often, dead with the overpowering weight of all the dead, it would so press against the partition of this next dimension that we should hear the mathematical wall crack.

And if with the violence of the Ichthian act you can plunge, when you are miserable, into the great world-substratum of death and press through this into the unknown dimension beyond, you can stand apart from the whole process by the act of de-carnation and turn yourself into a pure disembodied consciousness, a consciousness that can hover not only outside the sensitized organism of your own bodily identity, but sufficiently apart from the whole astronomical spectacle as to be able to regard it with a measure of detachment.

It seems a peculiarity of human nature that we can bear up better under sudden tragic disasters than under the normal pressure of the dreary, the squalid, the futile, the commonplace; and it is in resistance to these things and against these things that it is necessary to acquire the habit of these two mental devices, the one giving us strength to plunge deeper into the reality of life and death, and the other enabling us to contemplate them both as it were from outside and with a certain curious aloofness.

To make all this clearer and more concrete for the reader of this book let me at this point suggest an only too possible actual situation. Allow me to assume that you are following a forlorn road in some district of some town where the houses are unappealing and where the shops and pavements have given place to that peculiar shoddiness that is only not quite so forbidding as the vulgarest kinds of suburban trimness.

As you advance you grow aware of that particular kind of dreariness hanging like a sour breath over all you see that would be impossible alike in the heart of a town and in the heart of the country. The vulgar neatness of prosperous new villas might be worse but in that case your nature would be roused to an angry distaste which at least would give you the satisfaction of something to hate. But here all is merely depressing, merely dreary, merely negligible and neutral.

Human life in this place with all its surroundings has an air of something reduced to so low an emphasis that it is like the languid movement of flies on a discoloured window-pane. What can a soul sensitive to external impressions, do to cope with the weight of desolation that weighs it down in such a spot? And suppose, in addition to these surroundings you are weary with the labour of some distasteful job, you have been unkindly treated by the companion of your life, your neighbours have been casting malicious aspersions upon you, and you have been only recently jeered at by someone or other. You are, let us presume, a kind of philosopher after your own fashion. At least you are not one to take your present misery for granted, or to give way to futile self-pity and useless repining. You feel in the last resort that everything happens to you only happens because you yourself by reason of the weakness of your mind, *let it happen*. What then are you to do? Well! This particularly wretched moment, perhaps more wretched because you cannot *hate* your life-companion or your neighbours, or the children who jeered at you, or this lack-lustre neutral spot, or even the weary tedium of your job, is a moment that lends itself beautifully to this fierce gathering-together of your deepest soul for what I call the Ichthian act.

But you are so weary, so sick to death of the daily struggle, that though you have managed to grub along somehow, as indeed you *have* to do whether you like it or not if you are to avoid the bread-line, it seems more than you can compass to invoke any spirit of enjoyment; and as for plunging into some other "dimension," it is all you can do not to raise up your hands and cry to the burden of the one around you, "Hold, enough!"

Well! never mind about the Ichthian act. Perhaps such a thing *is* only for those to whom Nature has given by temperament a certain kind of defiant energy. But, listen! We all have our own poor modicum of what people call intelligence. Let us see what can be done with that. Here you are, fairly landed in a net-work of fatality—and though ill luck has certainly played its part, the un-wisdom of your decisions, the weakness of your will, have played their part too.

Well! tired and sick of the whole business as you are, it does remain that you're not yet prepared to commit suicide. Even in your weariness, potent though the devil is in such conditions, you don't feel like ending it. Something, some natural human instinct, holds you back from the thought of killing yourself, and, besides, at the very bottom of your organism stirs still that holy spawn of the last ditch that mortals call hope. But what of the great philosophers? Can *they* help at this juncture?

The worst of the great philosophers is that they each offer their particular nostrum as if it were the only way. Life is so manifold that in reality there are many ways of salvation! Secretly, in their own private life, we may suspect that Socrates and Epicurus and Epictetus and Marcus Aurelius, and even the formidable Spinoza, had recourse, when they were harassed by circumstances, to all sorts of mental devices quite other than the particular panacea they publicly recommend. With all moralists and philosophers there enters a special kind of egoism which commits them to a particular line of argument. What inspires their books is really the angel-demon of their temperamental fatality. This is their initial and original vision; and their superiority consists in the depth of this flash of primary insight, an insight generally reached, as William James hints, in one superb movement of imaginative reason. But such is the massive and sturdy egoism of these powerful brains that having once snatched at their one inspired *aperçu,* they proceed for all the rest of their lives to prop it up and thicken it out by logical reason. And reason, being the thing it is, never as wise as mother-wit, never as inspired as imagination, sees to it that having once committed themselves to their particular cosmic clue, these thinkers keep on to the end, justifying it, defending it; scared above everything of confessing that their original vision of things might possibly have grown *into something completely different* had their experience of life found them with a more flexible mind.

What, in personal experience, makes us wise is a certain steadiness of temper combined with a certain daring of thought, a daring that is prepared to practice any number of "volte-faces."

It is for this reason that wayward spirits like Kwang-Tze, or inspired soothsayers like Heraclitus, or great imaginative intellects like Dostoievsky, convey in their casual utterances so much more of the vital sap of the secret of life than all the rational rounders-off of logical systems. Behind each of the great philosophic systems, as William James so wonderfully hints, lies the personal "will to believe" of the particular thinker, a "will to believe" that very likely had its origin in precisely the sort of desperate struggle against depression upon which you are now engaged.

At this moment, if you are a reader, you will probably catch yourself suppressing some rebellious or wayward or paradoxical thought of your own,

— 43 —

and trying pathetically to force the situation into the perspective of some Nietzschean or Goethean vision of things, which does not fit the occasion.

When, therefore, you feel too weary of life to resist your misery I am not going to suggest that my own private panacea is the *only* way out. Like that poor preacher whom Matthew Arnold met in Bethnal Green when all seemed hopeless, there are persons still to-day who can pull themselves up from the pit with a sublime jerk, as if by their own belts, in the thought of "Christ, the living Bread." Well! If *this* magic is possible to you, for heaven's sake use it!

To confess the truth I have myself once and again—and not so long ago either—pulled myself out of the Slough of Despond by the old religious incantations. I only allude to this as an indication that from my own point of view the more con- juring tricks we have in our pilgrim's wallet the better, and that I have no fanatical preference for *my* favourite magic over all the rest.

I am anxious however in this first chapter to reduce my subject to its most stripped and primor- dial terms; and brought down thus to the bed-rock of human experience, what we are all confronted with is the necessity for *some* magic of the mind if we are to escape the pressure upon us of these dark hours when the burden of our normal existence seems more than we can endure. And where what I call the Ichthian act—though there are doubtless many other restorative tricks of the persecuted spirit—has the advantage in its trick of gathering into one grand cloud of evil *all* our mental and physical discomfort. And this it does by stripping the situation of all particular causes of worry and pain, until what we have left is the individual soul confronted by a world composed *in the lump* of suffering-bringing elements. A few of the worst of these must be simply "forgotten"—and the forgetting power within the soul is the gods' greatest gift to man—but the bulk of them must simply be lumped together.

It is certainly advisable to recall the precept, "In the destructive element immerse!" only we must recall it with deep reservations, for it is not given to any mortal man to face *all* and live.

Let me recapitulate a little so as to make each step of this particular technique as clear as I can. The unlucky person I have had in mind all this while as a typical example of our common lot finds himself, or herself, as I have said, confronted by objects of almost unredeemed forlornness, not desolate enough to reach what might be called the sublime of desolation, but so dreary, miserable, meaningless and commonplace, as to dry up the soul with a sick revulsion from the whole business of being alive.

The person in question has been hurt by the unkindness or driven to the end of his tether by the unhappiness, of his nearest and dearest. He has been outraged by his neighbours. He has been jeered at by the heartlessness of the young. He has come to loathe his job. He finds himself spiritless and exhausted; all the magnetism in him drained away, all his energy, all his resistance, gone.

As I suggested above, it is likely enough at such a moment that if he thinks of the words of moralists and philosophers at all he will either repeat to himself some ponderous tag against the weight of which all that is original in him rises in rebellion or he gives it up and allows the waves of depression to sweep over him at their will.

But, instead of this, let him "lump" all his evils together and contemplate them in the mass. Here he sees, in his spiritless apathy, a lumped-together world, composed of a mass of hurting reality and a few flickering will-o'-the-wisps of barely conceivable enjoyment.

It is into this mingled world-mass, into this compound of much wretchedness and a few oases of pleasure that the soul plunges, in what I call the Ichthian act; plunges into it, and then, with a terrific leap, plunges into the unknown dimension above it and around it.

But, as I say, if you have lost your zest for living how can you "plunge" anywhere? You lack the spirit. You can only rest where you are in sullen protest. If you were not driven from your bed at this moment, what would suit you best would be to lie there forever, with your eyes shut, without thought, or power, or memory, or aim, enjoying the pleasure of death without the shock of dying.

But—"whoever you are," as Walt Whitman used to say, though I will not raise my voice to his disquieting pitch—what I am recommending to you now is my second redemptive trick, the one I have named de-carnation. Project your soul from your troubled brain, *or pretend to yourself that you project it,* and from its new position in the air by your side let it watch you and your misery!

I entirely agree with you that most spiritual efforts by which we either give up our will or exert our will, either pull ourselves together, or relax ourselves completely, are anything but easy to achieve. They require constant practice, over long periods of time, and they require, just as my Ichthian act does, a certain elasticity of mind if not a certain resistance of vitality. We have to "have the heart" for such experiments before we can make them; and what you feel at this second of time is no heart for anything. Nevertheless, wearily and inertly, using no effort except the mere movement of thought, you can at least lump your many worries and your many miseries together; and when you have done so pretend to project your soul into the air at your side. From this aloofness to it all, then, and still as wearily as you please—for, there is a faint, weird element of self-pleasing in all inertness—contemplate this pain-causing lumped-together universe.

Here is your soul, like a broken-winged Space-Bird, watching cursorily this bubble of an earth-life; watching it without love, without hate, without curiosity—just watching it in weary detachment. Watch it a little longer now, O persecuted soul, just one second longer, and you will perceive, if I am not mistaken, a mysterious feeling, slowly, very slowly, beginning to take possession of you. It is as though a strange sort of trance were stealing over your senses, a waking-trance that will soon become, if you continue staring at this lumped-together world, a sensation as if you were waiting, along with the whole universe, for some withheld clue.

Suddenly—without realizing that you have already escaped from the worst of your personal misery—you will feel aware that this piled-up cosmic mass in front of you shares your plight. As you go on watching it, it will seem to be, this whole inanimate world, in as sad a case as your own. You have hynotized yourself in fact by staring at this lumped-together world with its implication of dumb expectancy, till you feel as if in your own trance-like state you were in touch with some strange universal endurance which is mutely appealing to you; appealing to you to share its sadness, and to share, with its sadness, its faint dim hope.

There is a line in Wordsworth—"The pleasure which there is in life itself"—which, if I may confess a personal secret, has been of singular value to me in moments of misery, but which I only use after I have made in it an extremely drastic change.

The line, as I have come to use it, runs as follows now, "The pleasure which there is in life and death;" and these words have been of an almost magical value to me in this altered form. I think it has conveyed to me a most important clue to the mysterious appeal which the inanimate has for you when you are unhappy. Compared with our own life-feeling, even in its saddest and most inert moods, the inanimate world of the non-human has a tragic helplessness which to us appears like a kind of death. And as we brood upon this mute *sub-life,* which to us seems so near to death, there arises in us a strange awe in the presence of its patience, of its dumb endurance.

Now it is from this particular kind of awe, when we are enduring these desolate moments, that I feel we can extract our comfort. In this mood we share the death-element in the world, that element out of which we come and into which, as far as our bodies are concerned, we sink, without having to make any nerve-shaking plunge. In the kind of waking-trance I have attempted to describe we approach by the mere numbness produced by our personal miseries this vast *sub-life* of the world, and feel already, without shock or strain, a state of being resembling the semi-death of the inanimate.

The state I am thinking of is, if you will, allied to despair; for like despair it throws into one huge tide of desolation all our lesser worries and discomforts, but it is unlike despair in the fact that while it numbs us and dulls us it does not close for us the gates of hope. We, like the vast "sub-life" of the inanimate, are waiting some clue to the mysterious illness of the world. Mute, helpless and silent, we await what has been awaited for so many unthinkable millions of years; and though no clue is given we at least feel we are sharing the "rooted sorrow" in the bones of life itself and are already dwelling in that strange no-man's land that lies beneath all human consciousness.

What we touch, as from this vantage-ground of our detached soul we contemplate life and death, is the universal ingredient in all human wretchedness, I mean in such wretchedness as stops short of extreme pain or of direct sympathy with extreme pain; and I feel as if I find what I am looking for in an amalgam of three evil things, all ending in the letter "y," Misery, Apathy, Worry. It is this devil's trinity, with this long-tailed she-demon of a "why" at the end of each member, that we have to attack at the root.

Stronger measures than any I have the power to tell of are naturally our resource when in extreme pain; but in this misery, in this worry, in this apathy, I do feel I may be able to suggest something that might work the desired end; and that, too, without resorting to the more energetic technique of what I call the Ichthian act.

The particular human attitude I am now suggesting resembles that of a patient beast with its rump against the weather, but with its conscious soul watching both the weather and its misery from a certain distance. I am imagining you, reader, in this woeful state, surrounded by all the sights which evoke the atmospheric condition known as "dreariness" and with all your private griefs thick upon you. Your spirit is so low that you wish you were dead, though you lack the heart to commit suicide.

If you had your desire it would be to lie down upon some solitary bed, away from every living person, and forget who you are or what you are, or that you have ever lived!

Well! In place of seeking such a bed of oblivion just try the experiment of "lumping together"—I have to keep repeating this clumsy expression—all your worry, misery, apathy in one evil mass of detestation and then from a detached soul watch both it and yourself with a curious eye.

You—a living human creature—produced by Nature and the First Cause—find yourself, by the blundering wickedness and careless weakness of humanity, stupefied with misery, dumb with apathy, paralysed with worry. But as you stand still for a moment and out of the air by your side allow your detached soul to stare at this amalgam of Troubles, and to stare at the forlorn objects about you you will find that these things when "lumped-together" are a completely different matter than they were in their separateness. The horrid separate objects dissolve into earth and air and water and fire, while your separate distresses dissolve into one single burden of distress; and as you watch this process you feel that something in your detached consciousness is outside it all and defiant of it all.

"This is you," as those staring advertisements of bright young men, pointing admonitory fingers, delight to remind us, "This is you." And indeed you might easily be standing now at this very second of time on some crowded pavement in Soho, on some East-Side Avenue in Manhattan, on some railway platform of the Loop in Chicago, in some forlorn suburb of London, or by the blackened edge of the old canal-river at Manchester. Yes, you might easily be going through this misery in any of these places, and as you stare at the oily water, at the soot-darkened boards, at the blackened stones, at the glaring advertisements, at the hard asphalt, at the hell-pavement of adamantine concrete, it may well happen that just because what is observing all this is nothing less than your *mind,* the creator and destroyer of the world, all this will "suffer a sea-change."

It is not, as we might have hoped, that all this will grow less substantial, or begin to vanish away under the detached scrutiny of your uncommitted consciousness. Rather will all this as your mind detaches itself from it grow more and more real. But it will grow real with the reality of earth, air, water, fire as these elements emphasize themselves and swallow up the dreariness.

And as in your weakness and your melancholy you still observe these things, these blackened boards, this oily water, these dirty windows, these sad chimneys, this harsh cement, you will feel in them only the ancient hardness of the earth, only the ancient emptiness of the air, only the ancient washing of the tides, only the ancient burning of the sun, and there will come over you the grand and sombre tragedy of all human life confronted by these things and of all these things confronted by human life, from the very beginning of the story.

And you will feel your own life with all that long procession of lives before it, and you will feel your own death with all that long procession of deaths before it, and by degrees these two awarenesses will blend in an emphasis you have never felt before, while the impress of the inanimate things about you, their forbidding *alienness* confronted by this pitiful oblong bundle of nerves which is yourself, will take on a different character.

Balanced thus in a perpendicular position among these things, your unhappy organism, shaped like a sausage, tied at the neck and at the waist with string, will feel through its fibres as your soul watches it the dim faint stir of an emotion that is not an altogether unhappy one!

The sense of a nobler, a more serious drama going on than you had guessed at is upon you now, and your future moments of misery will come to you with a difference. While you were watching your own lumped-together miseries and the lumped-together inanimates of desolation around you, you touched the bed-rock bottom of the world. On that dark glass—harder than despair itself—you tapped with your forehead and though there was no answer to your tapping, simply to have tapped was something.

"The Pleasure which there is in life and death" flowed through you at that moment, and a curious awareness of something in your mind outside the whole game.

Though you lacked the spirit to make the Ichthian leap, you did manage the act of "de-carnation"; and as you hovered and wavered in your humming sea of misery—apathy—worry, watching your perpendicular self, like a poor drowned sausage tied at the neck and the waist with string, bobbing up and down, you clutched a shell of pure Mother-of-Pearl, the pleasure which there is in Life and Death at the very bottom of the world!

LET CONSCIENCE SPEAK

---

*This thing called Conscience—Giving way to Misery—
The universe as a battle-ground—Heightening our
mental life—The Panergic act—The little-great compensating pleasures — A concrete example — The
world's pain—Hugging our unhappiness.*

THERE COME MOMENTS IN ALL OUR LIVES WHEN
we say to ourselves, "What does it matter whether I
feel happy or not?" Now this mood is of all moods
the most insidious and dangerous. The next step is
to say to ourselves, "I will, I will, I *will* be unhappy!" And it is then that we begin giving ourselves up to that dark under-flow of *the will to
destruction,* which, if it does not exist in the nature
of the First Cause—as it sometimes seems to do—
certainly exists, as an appalling and most real element, in the nature of all men and women.

The moment our relations with other souls enters
the arena what we call our "conscience" becomes
active enough. It is when we are alone that this particular danger arises, the danger of being obsessed
by the Power of Self-Destruction.

So deep is the mandate of conscience, do what we can, in every human heart, that in all matters of external behaviour few things play a more fatal part, but a great many people allow themselves to go on being miserable simply because, while they use their conscience in other relations of life, something prevents their using it in this crucial personal sense.

I am introducing this question thus early in my book because I feel that everything else is of secondary importance in the art of happiness compared with this fundamental matter. Our conscience is always forcing us to make the necessary efforts to get through our work, to behave decently to others, to avoid cruelty, greediness, laziness, treachery and lying, but somehow it seems to require some startling shock, such as the menace of insanity, to rouse us to the recognition that at the root of our whole response to life there lies the question, "Why do we let ourselves go on being miserable when it is in the power of our mind to alter our state?" In matters of conscience it is always harder to strike down to the buried secrets of our feeling than to obey the impulse to *do* something or other; and as to this matter of cultivating, or refusing to cultivate, a living spring of happiness in our deeper nature, it seems as if most of us were quite prepared to let the whole thing go, as long as we get through life and get through our work somehow.

Thus we drift on, living a higgledy-piggledy sort of existence, or just one of those dreary lives of monotonous necessity, when the mind gets so dyed-in-the-grain by petty cares, and so stupefied by taking such a state for granted, that it lacks even the intermittent glow of relief of not being, at the actual moment, in pain or cold or hunger.

Heraclitus was right. Life is war, down to the very bottom. And that is why it is a treacherous and devilish argument to say to the enemies of military war that the masses need stirring up to heroism. The majority of human beings on this earth—not only women bearing and looking after children, but men at their most ordinary and most monotonous jobs— have all the scope any hero needs, any saint needs, for rising to spiritual heights of sublime intensity.

This thing called "conscience," that is such a tormentor to us all, may, as I have hinted, be the edge-of-the-wedge of the terrible force of Evolution, pressed with a burning electric spear-head against our vitals, to compel us to bestir ourselves and live vitally and intensely from the focus-point of our nature.

But whatever our conscience may be I think we would all have to confess that it changes its imperatives as it comes under new influences. The conscience grows as other living things grow, and it can be blighted and withered as they can; and what I would like to point out here is that in all the great spiritual teachers from Laotze to Spinoza the chief stress is laid upon what you are feeling in the secret depths of your own soul rather than upon exterior actions.

The greatest among the mediaeval saints always laid this same stress on the feelings of the soul as against any outward manifestation and the whole quarrel between Laotze's interpreter, the wayward and wind-loving Kwang-Tze and the ritualistic Confucius, was that the former insisted that nothing mattered in this question of virtue but the flowing water and the wavering air of the soul's own secret life.

There is indeed, all the way down the ages, a secret free-masonry, passed from mouth to mouth among certain great teachers, laying this same stress upon the inner feelings of the soul as against outward actions.

Some philosophers even go so far as to hold the view that if you habitually indulge in deep secret malicious thoughts with regard to a particular person you can seriously injure that person; but if the mood of your deepest soul is on the side of evil when it indulges in hate, it is equally on the side of evil when it indulges in what the mediaeval schoolmen called "acedia," that destructive self-malice which pours poison into the wellspring of our own soul.

There are two ways in which the magic of life can be brought low. It can be beaten down from outside by brutal tyranny; and it can be weakened at the root by this soft and melancholy worm of self-malice. There is no doubt that psychic vibrations of some kind emanate from all our moods. Not even the most rigid materialist can gainsay this. And when a person allows himself to be unhappy day after day and year after year, what he is really doing is helping the spirit of evil.

Can it be that there is a vein of this self-destructive *unhappiness* in the nature of the First Cause itself? Is it *this* that is behind that look of unspeakable self-pity that you catch sometimes upon the face of inanimate things? What else is that solemn sadness of old trees, old hill-sides, old twisted rain-beaten thorns, old grassy slopes, old pond-sides, old desolate valleys unvisited by birds or cattle?

There is a strange connection between us and the life of the planet that gave us birth and when we give way hour by hour and day by day to the misery of futility we betray our ancient accomplices in the mysterious drama. We drag down the confederate spirit in stones and trees. We burden the wind, we darken the sun, we trouble the air, we deepen the moan of the sea.

And if there is a link between us and these primordial existences, how much more between us and the mass of our fellows? Them also, those we touch, those we pass by, those even we know nothing of, we help by our hopelessness to drag down! They feel our inertness, our secret misery, our burden of futility, and for them too, because of our existence, the weight of life grows heavier, the dawns rise more darkly, the twilights fall more sadly, the night-winds are more desolate and lost.

There is undoubtedly something, in our abandonment to misery, of an evil and destructive satisfaction. It is a dark negative satisfaction. It is scarcely pleasure! But undoubtedly there are vibrations of despair, auras of life-hatred, atmospheres of dissolution, motions of destruction, abroad upon our air, the air that has been breathed for so many thousands of years by men like ourselves; and when a soul gives itself to misery it is not isolated, it is not alone. Dark destructive forces, spiritual as well as chemical, are there to be tapped and drawn upon.

We all live our life amid powers dimly discerned, amid presences and influences that hang about our path and dog our steps. Once give way to a certain kind of misery and you draw these influences to yourself. You go about like one obsessed, and you *are* obsessed. We are all Dramatis Personae in a vast deep tragical Play, of which we know neither the beginning nor the end. We all live in an invisible as well as a visible world and between these worlds there are more communications than we guess. The whole cosmos, visible and invisible, is a battle-ground of warring spirits. Nature herself has something in her of inexplicable evil, something in her that drags downward, that feeds on dissolution, something lemur-like and wraith-like that lives on the dead. And this unfathomable battle-field is full of ancient arenas of disaster. Terrible waste-lands and ghastly no-man's lands are there, with old milestones of defeats, old stakes of death, old rags of lost and discoloured banners drooping over pits of the forgotten slain.

No man knows the issue of it. None have seen the "High Command" on either side. There seems no "High Command" at all. There only seems on one hand a blind dim multitudinous stirring and heaving towards the light, and on the other a wild, chaotic, panic-rout, drifting towards the darkness.

And this battle-field of the unfathomable cosmos is composed of minds, of thoughts, of the inner life of nerves. What we call the objective Universe, what we call the Nature, are things quite as much *created* by the innumerable minds that throng them as they are things discovered by these.

Nature to man is one thing. To a beast, to a fish, to a bird it is another thing. To an elemental of the air it is yet another thing! And who shall say which is the reality? Yes, the cosmic battle-field is a battle-field of mental forces, clashing upon mental levels. No two human beings see the same "real universe." There is no real universe. There are as many "universes" as there are minds. Something, some mysterious "field of intercourse," holds all these separate universes together, and this "field of intercourse," this meeting-ground of mental worlds, is the battle-field of our life. A battle-ground? It is a phantom-ground of inexplicable mystery, across which old terrible death-cries of defeat, and old terrible exultation-cries of victory go tossing and wailing by on eternally recurrent winds.

The new conquest of the air in our generation, in this beginning of what our astrologers call "the Aquarian Age," is a material symbol of the communication that has always been taking place—though only realized by a few soothsayers and poets—between all the bewildered offspring of our doomed planet. There have always been "wireless" interchanges, as the battle between the forces of destruction and the forces of creation ebbed and flowed, between all the "poor creatures of earth." We need no St. Paul to tell us that "the whole creation groaneth and travaileth in pain together" until now. There have always been sun-obsessed souls and moon-obsessed souls, always been human entities ridden by the forces of destruction, inspired by the forces of creation. There have always been

human entities closer to the earth, closer to the inanimate, both for good and evil, than others. This
outward world of the five senses is a thing upon
which the inner world of conscious minds is forever
working miracles.

War? Not a second of our days passes when we
are not in a state of life-and-death struggle, when
we are not being depressed by the down-drag of
defeat or inspired by the electricity of victory.

What we call our "conscience" is the sentinel at
the gate of the dark tower of the soul's besieged
fortress. There is treachery within the gate, there is
a traitor within the walls, when we regard our unhappiness as our destiny.

If our "conscience" does not rise up in indignation
at our submission to our misery it is a devil-ridden
and evil-mastered conscience. Every time you make
the required effort and force yourself to be happy
rather than unhappy you are helping to create the
world. Every time you refuse this effort and hug
your misery in that mood of dark complicated self-
malice you are helping to destroy the world.

Let no man say it matters nothing whether you
are happy or not as long as you labour for the cause
of your country or the cause of your humanity. It is
a lie! It is the devil speaking, though he speak "with
the tongues of angels."

The cause of your country and the cause of humanity are nothing compared with *the cause of the cosmos*. There are forces at war here far deeper, far more important, than whether communism overcomes capitalism or fascism overcomes democracy.

The old religious people were perfectly right in making the individual soul a microcosm of the whole. Let your soul be a microcosm, not a micropolis, not a necropolis!

Every time you gather the powers of your soul together and force yourself to be interiorly happy in the face of overpowering evils you are fighting the battle of creation against destruction.

No matter that none sees you, that none knows what is happening. The greatest struggles in the long tragic history of humanity, all down the ages, have been, in spite of what "fame" may say, *invisible struggles,* "known only," as the old religious people used to say, "to yourself and God."

What is not sufficiently realised is that the whole drama of life goes on in individual minds, and is independent of outward actions and outward events. Our life is lived in a *mental world* whereof the material background is forever changing according to the mood of the individual mind.

And this does not only apply to imaginative or intellectual people. It applies to everyone! We may present the appearance of "forked radishes," or of sausages tied at the neck and waist, or of scarecrows on perambulating sticks, or of fancy dolls, or of phantom-masks of tragedy. From the round knobs on the top of us there look forth upon the world those terrible holes into eternity that we call human eyes and what you see at the bottom of these holes is the world of mind, a world full of pits that go down into hell and of corridors leading to paradise.

It is one of the conceited illusions of intellectual people that they alone live an imaginative life. Everyone lives an imaginative life in the sense that everyone half-creates by his peculiar nerves and temperament the constitution of the material world he confronts.

It is extraordinary, when you really think of it, how few people there are who make any habitual effort to deal deliberately and intensely with their secret reactions to life. We live in a perpetual pathetic hope that things are going to be "better," which means outwardly nicer and outwardly pleasanter for us. We lavish our energy on plans to improve our condition but seldom concentrate it on heightening our mental reaction to the moment as it passes.

And yet everything else is of minor importance to this. Even our conscience—that formidable tyrant of our *actions*—is slack and feeble when it comes to our thoughts. The innumerable hours we spend on self-pity or on building castles in the air wherein to enjoy ourselves is a proof of this.

We ought to get it lodged in our conscience that the noblest, greatest, highest, deepest obligation we have, our one grand piety, our supreme return to the cosmos for giving us consciousness, is to heighten our mental life from moment to moment. And the heightening of our mental life means rousing up of our whole nature to defy and to enjoy, to defy the evil things, to enjoy the good things, to act as a destroyer and a creator in our secret consciousness. When you do this, when your soul gathers itself together to force your surroundings to respond to its resolute will it puts itself in sympathy with the whole creative life-tide and in opposition to the Ancient Antagonist. Is not this a thing worthy of the human conscience?

When you realise that the whole drama is a mental drama, and that the whole poignancy of it and tragic grandeur of it lies in these secret mental struggles with the demons of worry, misery, apathy, you realise that you are an important "Persona"— as important as any other living soul—in the great eternal tragic play. And what is more, you not only tap the invisible life-stream, as against the death-pull downwards, you feel yourself in a strange magnetic contact with the life-aura of uncountable numbers of fellow-creatures, dead and forgotten before you were born to carry on the torch, fellow-creatures who in their day wrestled with apathy, misery and worry, and whose magnetic energy lives still in the elements around you.

Every time when in dreary and depressing conditions you refuse to yield to the death-pull you associate yourself with a multitudinous army of stout hearts, most of whom have borne worse things than you will ever have to bear.

Not a moment of your life, when, from the magic of those mysterious aspects of the universe which appeal to your particular human senses your soul has roused itself to snatch its secret joy, is lost in futility. The great secret tragic play of the mental world of our race lies behind this moment's triumph, giving it an eternal significance. Because of this rousing of your inmost identity to defy the death-pull and to enjoy the unfathomable pleasure which your soul half-creates and half-discovers, you have added something to the reality of existence *which will always remain.*

Vibrations will pass from it, are even now passing from it, that will long outlive you.

The mental life of the whole human race resembles the accumulative invisible Novel of a super-Dostoievsky, heavy with an unfathomable burden of good and evil; and every moment in which your soul rises up from the depths of its being and defies these accurst devils of misery, worry and apathy, you add something that helps to determine the grand invisible drift of this cosmic work of art. What we call reality has many layers of various and differing degrees of intensity. The visible world, since it changes according to the eye or according to the mood that regards it, is less "real" than our intense inner life of thought, while our inner life of thought is itself less "real" than the unknown dimension that surrounds and includes it.

What I have called the Ichthian act is a desperate mental gesture, like the leap of a fish into the air, carrying us for an infinitesimal second beyond our normal self into that portion of our identity that remains at least sufficiently outside the astronomical universe to make us know for certain that *this is not all there is*.

What I have called "the act of de-carnation" is another desperate gesture of the mind by which we project, or intensely pretend that we project, our conscious soul "to a place in space at our side," from which we can survey in curious detachment our agitated physical organism and all its troubles.

Now, however, I have reached a point when I must strain my reader's patience to the uttermost by begging him to let me make use of a third invented name to emphasize a less desperate and more normal movement of the soul. I have no doubt that the use of these fancy words will be peculiarly irritating to the type of human mind always inimical to my own; but this book is nothing if it isn't an attempt to hand over to others the particular mental tricks that at a pinch have best served my own turn, and I have always found the opinion of the old magicians to be true that you get an advantage over a thing—whether angelic or demonic—the moment you can name it. Where would psychoanalysis be, for instance, without its curious language?

In Shakespeare's time you often had to invent words for certain poetical feelings. In our time, in this beginning of the "Aquarian Age," you have to invent words for psychological feelings.

Well, the word I am going to use for this calmer and less desperate gathering together of the forces of the soul is the word "Panergic," and I use this word not only because of its richly satisfying sound but because just as with "Ichthian" I brought in a Catacomb-Christian allusion, and with "de-carnation" a breath of those old Gnostic Heresies that have always fascinated me, so with "Panergic" I remind myself of that mysteriously alluring and most significant expression of Aristotle's, "Energeia Akinesis," which, though applied by him to the nature of the Deity, can I think without presumption be applied to all living minds.

It would be a great disappointment to me if this small treatise on what, after all, is the most important personal matter in human life, were only to appeal to that exclusive minority—not by any means always the wisest among us—that we have come to call the "Intelligentsia," and so I hope to be able to make clear what I mean by the "Panergic act" without having recourse to any elaborate metaphysical justification of the term. It is a beautiful word and a pleasant-sounding word; and, if I can make plain what I am driving at in using it, it will have served my turn well enough.

The truth is that the simplest of us know how often we are vexed and ashamed by the pettiness and tiresomeness of our thoughts when we are not engaged in absorbing labour or distracting play. A worker or a peasant who has spent unfairly long hours at his job has the best excuse for allowing his thoughts to fall into a series of irrelevant wanderings, giving him no pleasure, doing him no good, not even (for they keep hovering round a thousand grievances and a thousand vexations) resting or relaxing his tired brain.

But if your working hours are reasonable, whether you work with head or hand, so that you are not dog-tired when they're over, it does, when you come to think of it, seem preposterous that you go on day by day letting them debouch here and there at random. I beg the readers of this book to just keep

an eye on their thoughts to-day, as they go to work
and return from work, or as they let their hands
drop from their machine, or their tool, or their
pen, or their needle, or their type-writer, in intervals
of their labour, and I believe they will, like myself
as I take my exercise, be shocked by the silliness and
vanity of the things round which these random
thoughts keep hovering.

Why is it that after all these long centuries of
human experience of earth-life while we have learnt
to be such adepts at everything else we are still so
helpless and babyish in the management of the most
important thing of all, the working of our own
mind?

I think it is because, while we have put *the imperative of conscience* behind everything else, we
have left our thoughts to their own stupid and tiresome devices.

What a thing the mind of a living person is—the
miracle of miracles, the god of gods! But into this
thrice-precious, this thrice-holy vessel we allow the
very litter and debris and offscouring of the world to
drift as it will, carried there by every wind that
blows.

And my secret impression is that we are all alike
in this, the ones with clever brains equally with the
most simple-minded. I believe we would be singu-
larly ashamed of most of our "great men" to-day, if

we could watch the bits of rubbish, the wind-blown straws of unmitigated silliness, that pass unrebuked in and out of those famous heads.

And it is not as though we were really "relaxing," as people call it, or resting our exhausted energies, when we make no attempt to stop these dung-beetle larvae, these flying ashes from the everlasting dust-cart, these prickly burrs, these fumes of the prison-house, these meaningless midges of memory, to find harbourage in a mind that has taken millions of galaxies of burning constellations, millions of miracles of chance and fatality to call into being. Many of the "thoughts"—what a word for these contemptible invaders!—that in our weakness we dally with are anything but soothing or peaceful. Very often we catch ourselves quite unconsciously, if I may use so gross a comparison, scratching our minds when they itch under these midgets.

Constantly we find ourselves wincing under the affliction. But most often we just give a sigh of shame when we discover the number of minutes that we have allowed ourselves to pick the wretched-est scraps of memory to pieces, or to build up the most meaningless mud-pies out of the wastelands of random observation. Heaven knows we become the slaves of our consciences in other things. Why can't we put into these terrible angels' heads to start one of their remorseless taboos, one of their ferocious campaigns, in regard to our random thoughts? Everybody knows how soon, how fatally soon, *a conscientious habit,* full of ridiculous exactions, gets complete mastery over us. When you consider that the real underlying drama of life, that tragic drama which is heavier with doom and richer with triumphant consummations than all our external historic events, takes place on the invisible mental plane, whereof the stage is the secret consciousness of men and women, does it not seem as though we were indeed under some inherited curse that we keep our conscience for what we *do* rather than for what we *think?*

Our religious ancestors had an advantage over us in that they believed in a Heavenly Eye that followed all their thoughts. But this advantage was spoilt for them by the extreme stupidity and narrow-minded jealousy of the brain behind this Eye. They felt, for instance, overwhelmed with shame if it caught them thinking lecherous thoughts; whereas of all classes of thoughts, if they are not of a sadistic character, that a sensible conscience would encourage rather than condemn, thoughts of an amorous or erotic character would rank second to few.

Our pious ancestors, feeling themselves under the All-seeing Eye, prided themselves on forcing their scattered thoughts to concentrate on God. I can well recall, in my Father's Somersetshire village, listening to the eloquent and extempore invocations at many a "Prayer-Meeting," as they used to be named, of our aged parish clerk, Mr. Childs. How the old man's uplifted hands used to shake, and what tears of emotion would roll down his bearded cheeks, as he prayed that "each and every one of us should think of high and heavenly things"!

This meant no doubt that this aged servant of God had it on his conscience in his moments of leisure to think of such matters as his redemption by Christ and his assurance of seeing his Redeemer with his own eyes after death.

Somewhat different, but not less remote from the visible world, are those "high and heavenly things" that mystics and idealists of all ages have been compelled by their consciences to ponder on, and to call on their disciples to ponder on. What were the thoughts of Socrates, when he fell into one of his famous trances, now on the battle-field, now in the streets of Athens, now on the threshold of some lively Symposium with his intellectual young men? What did his "conscience" call upon him to brood on beyond the beauty of Alcibiades? No doubt upon that super-dimension of loveliness and reality that he felt to be the abiding essence of the transitory glories of this mortal world.

And what for the great Plato were these "high and heavenly things," corresponding to the old

Montacute clerk's meditations on his redemption
through Christ? What were, in actual fact, the mental
images that this greatest of idealists felt upon his
conscience to summon up as he walked home to his
treasured collection of the "sayings" of Parmenides
from his own lectures in the Academia? Vague
poetical essences, may we not suppose they were,
wherein, under the form of "ideas," fairer rivers
than the waters of the Ilissus, lovelier divinities than
looked down on him from the Parthenon, more
gracious youths than ever listened to his teaching in
the Academia, revealed to his imaginative reason
what, especially for those fortunate souls who had
been purified in the "Mysteries," the Beyond-Life
held of unspeakable perfection?

"So much poppycock!" the sturdy tribe of Lucretius will exclaim, "all Moonshine, all Midsum-
mer Madness!"

Personally I take a different view. I hold that although our aged clerk's homely thoughts of his redemption by the Blood of the Lamb are not *exactly*
corresponded to by any secret cosmic truth, and
although Plato's "Back-of-the-World," full of invisible archetypes a thousand times more fair than
their broken and mirrored images in our present
experience, does not exactly answer to the truth of
things, yet there is an element of genuine corre-
spondency in them both, representing something at

variance with the science of any Lucretius and yet a real aspect of life.

But what I am now suggesting as the kind of subjects upon which our modern conscience, changed a little from both the metaphysical conscience of Plato and the evangelical conscience of Mr. Childs, would do well to command us to think, for I am as frightened, in the presence of the censorship of modern enlightenment, of referring to St. Paul's words upon this subject as St. Paul himself was of mentioning fornication, are matters much less ideal.

What my idea of the "Panergic act" amounts to in fact, if you can only get your conscience into the habit of commanding it, is an emphatic gathering up before your mind of those little-great compensating pleasures which make your existence bearable.

There are naturally occasions when it seems a kind of mockery to try to think of such things; and if you are, let us suppose, a harassed woman with many children, an over-worked charwoman, say, driven to the end of your tether by worry and anxiety, it is likely enough that all you can possibly do is to get through each day, as it comes, as stoically as you can. The same thing must, I fear, apply often in these times to many a man without work watching helplessly some child or wife of his, in worse health perhaps than himself, struggling against desperate odds to keep some job which undermines both body and spirit.

It is obvious that all a person can do in a book like this is to suggest certain mental tricks and palliatives for those luckier people who are not yet quite at the end of their tether, and who, while grimly holding on with all the strength they have, do still possess some measure of mental detachment wherewith to contemplate their state.

It is clear that if you are an over-burdened charwoman, or if you are a man out-of-work whose child, who *has* a job, is suddenly menaced with consumption as the result of this job, you may well enquire bitterly enough, "What is the cosmos to me? What is Conscience to me? What is all this talk about "Ichthian" acts and "Panergic" acts to me?

Well, I must confess that under these extreme conditions just as under the pressure of extreme pain, all human panaceas tend to seem an ironical mockery, an adding of insult to injury.

Probably at such times, unless you are a superhuman philosopher, your mental shifts and devices will have to suspend operations until chance, or death, or the aid of someone, more practical if not more Christian than any philosopher, comes to your rescue. Till then the utmost you can do is to hold on without getting drunk or committing suicide.

But let me assume that your case is not quite so

bad as this, not so bad, at any rate, for it to be a ghastly mockery for anyone to mention happiness in your presence.

Let me assume that you are dreading some particular interview with someone on the subject of money, an interview upon which you feel your fate depends, but which is, of all things in the world, the hardest for your peculiar disposition to face.

Or let me assume that you are preparing to undertake some responsible task the accomplishment of which seems to you insecure, uncertain, doubtful; some task in which you will have to keep your wits about you if you are not to be miserably humiliated, some task which, if you fail to carry it off, will bring about the loss of your berth, some task in which you will be forced to "bluff," but will be in devilish danger of having your bluff exposed!

Of course it would be possible to go on forever giving examples of the agitating crises that are always occurring, even in the most uneventful lives; but, whatever they may be, it is in view of the nervous misery of such situations as these, easy perhaps for others, but well-nigh intolerable to us, that a few crafty mental tricks might well be called on, to apply a modicum of soothing ointment to our spirit.

And in my opinion the mental gesture of intensely envisaging and holding tight to the particular great little pleasures that have most heightened your life is of the utmost value here, though I feel you have to think of these things in a rather especial way. Let me give you a concrete example of what I mean. You are, let us suppose, even now walking to the place where you have to face your doom, one way or the other, in this miserable responsibility. Dark and wet with rain are the grass-patches you pass and the smoke-blackened hedges have those sticky little leaves on them that so thrilled Ivan Karamazov. And your human-mind, that it has taken millions of constellations to bring to birth, and which, once born, may never, according to the great Pantagruel, "be cut off by Atropos' scissors," is so miserably occupied by nervous fears that for its dear life it cannot inhale a moiety of healing dew from this rain-dark grass or snatch the least flicker of joy from those sticky leaves, magical as the spittle of Jesus.

But come now! Drive your mind deeper and further than this frightful immediate responsibility that so hangs over you. Treat it *as if it were much worse than it is*. Treat it as if it might kill you. Look at these wet grass-blades as if for the last time. Yes, you are going to die, going to lie dead and cold with everything over.

Well! When you *do* die, as a result of facing this business, just remember these sticky leaf-buds! Look at them closely now, so as to have them in your mind when this affair finishes you off.

I tell you the foundation-stone of all human happiness is the thought of death. Gather your thoughts together therefore as you would do if you were going to your execution. In one swift motion of your mind think of all the things that have meant most to you. Face to face with your imaginary death you mentally clutch tight at the person you really love the most, seize for the last time, the poignancy and pathos of this person's existence, and then you snatch with a terribly swift snatch all this magic of earth and air and sunlight and rain that you are leaving.

And still moving forward to the place of your humiliation and death you now proceed to bid an everlasting farewell to all those little homely pleasures that have made life tolerable to you, all those moments when you have been happy over your book, happy over your food, happy over your fire, happy over your drink, happy as you smoked and read your paper, happy as you dug in your garden, happy as you turned over to sleep in your bed! Swiftly—for thought is swifter than light—you make an inevitable selection from these things, and, as you make this selection, all these things, your one great love and your little pleasures, will take on that tragic heightening that the approach of death alone can give.

And holding your death vividly in your consciousness gather your spirit together to face this appalling crisis.

It is a grotesque weakness at the very moment when you are holding death itself back at arm's length, *as we all are,* to be in such a plight because of a situation that at the worst will not do worse than humble you to the dust. This "Panergic" act of mine is not any desperate leap into some unknown dimension. It is no frantic escape of your consciousness from your body. I will tell you what it is. It is the supreme gesture of your bed-rock sense of proportion as to the relation between worry and death.

The great thing is to bring your conscience to bear on this whole matter. The human conscience is already, at least among a large minority, issuing its imperatives to us to refine upon our sense of beauty, to pursue truth, to cultivate kindliness and goodness, but it has not yet, except in a kind of intermittent accidental way here and there, taken upon itself to command us *to force ourselves to be happier than we are* especially in crucial and difficult circumstances.

What we call pleasure comes and goes but the Panergic act implies a recognition that all the living organisms of our race are struggling against vicious odds. Every moment you force yourself to be happy in spite of all you let loose upon the invisible world of human minds a current of magnetic force upon which—whether you know it or not or whether *they* know it or not—others instinctively draw.

The truth is, happiness of this kind has not yet been properly defined. It is as spiritual as it is sensuous, as intellectual as it is nervous. It is an acceptance of both life and death as things that culminate in a mental war, a war against misery, apathy, worry and futility. It is a movement of the mind by which you isolate the things that most especially thrill you out of all the rest, and hold them up, as it were before you, and clutch them to your spirit.

The ground of this Panergic embrace of the things that you are born to enjoy, things like food and drink and love and sleep and the magic of the elements and reading of exciting books and the fitful expressions on the face of nature, and the motley spectacle of the streets of towns, is your sense of the weight of the multitudes of the dead behind you, calling upon you to fill up the quota of such as overcome futility.

We all have sooner or later to face the ultimate question, "How have any of us a right to be happy at all, still less to make an art of happiness when so many fellow-organisms, both human and animal, are enduring unthinkable anguish?" And this question goes, I fully admit it, to the deep root of our whole problem. There are times when we feel so appalled by the atrocities of life that we feel as if the only possible existence for a sensitive spirit were to be a monk or a nun.

But you must remember you are after all a man, a woman, with a temperament organized by Nature to fight for happiness.

Goethe hints somewhere that Nature herself feels and is conscious through our individual minds; but it is not so much that we, to use a malicious and un-Goethean image, are like the happiness-feelers of the great cosmic cuttle-fish, as that we are an organic portion of the old familiar planet that gave us birth.

Between us and the living body of our mother the earth there often seems to stir strange reciprocities and it may easily be that our happiest moments come when between our human magnetism and the earth-magnetism there is established a mysterious harmony.

But though it sometimes seems as if our happiness drew us near to the earth, our pain seems to separate us from her.

If at any moment a sensitive person were made fully conscious of the appalling pain in the world he would go mad and die howling. The creative force however has taken effective measures that this should not happen and we are protected from it by our selfishness and stupidity. Indeed the wonder is not so much that we can go on living and being happy with all these atrocious sufferings around us as that there should ever have entered this world at all the sympathetic nerve by which we suffer with those that we see suffering.

On the other hand there comes a point when it is necessary to fall back upon our natural egoism if we are to live at all. What is the use of shirking the plain fact that, save in the cases of a few devoted lovers and mates, and a few devoted parents and children, we are all bound to be, intended to be, allowed to be, privileged to be, *and cannot help being,* lonely and self-centred egoists?

In all these ultimate partings-of-the-ways there is something a little shocking and ghastly about an attempt to carry things to logical extremes. Life over-brims logic in every direction but we cannot escape facing this matter of the desirability of forcing ourselves to feel sensations of happiness while people we know, and people we see, and people we read about, are suffering abominably.

It is hard to avoid the conclusion that although insensitive and stupid people have to be startled out of their selfishness the more sympathetic your nerves are and the more vivid your imagination is, the more necessary is it for you to have it on your conscience to force yourself to be happy against the grain of your nature if you are not to slide into a hopeless despair. For if we are not permitted to be thus happy, either by the tender indulgence of the great poppy-strewing Mother of us all or by our own mental effort, it becomes a logical impossibility for any child of Adam to be happy at all, *even for one single second*. For at every moment when someone is being happy—and this alas! is not a fantasy but an unquestionable fact—someone else is enduring an anguish that we shrink from imagining.

Most of us never grow quite callous. We do something. We lift a finger; we give a penny; but Nature herself sees to it that we do not have to struggle very hard to remain sturdily selfish! But here we are, with the evil in the universe pressing down on all of us, on some devilishly, on some heavily, on all a little. No external event is completely under our control. Few are under our control at all. And as we go from our room to our work, or from our bed to our kitchen-grate we find ourself surrounded by all the contrarieties of the cosmos.

On every side are sights that are grotesque, ironical, monstrous, meaningless, harsh, ugly, infinitely sad, infinitely heart-breaking, and yet touched, all of them, now and again by a magical beauty. Most of these things of whatever kind they are, are beyond our power of altering. What is there that we *can* alter or control? Certainly not, it would seem, the character of our mate, of the companion of our bed and board! His or her secret thoughts escape us completely even as our own escape his.

What can we do that is beyond the power of man, or god, or chance or fate, to stop our doing? What can we do that will be our inmost private personal response to the mysterious Cosmos that has given us our life?

Well, *we can be unhappy.* We can be unselfishly unhappy, brooding in our imagination and in our nerves on the anguish felt at this moment by someone else, and we can be selfishly unhappy, brooding upon our own miseries, apathies, worries, upon our own grievances and ailments, upon our own wrongs; or *we can force ourselves to be happy.* These alternatives are within our power when nothing else is within our power. And it seems to me that it is sheer madness to let our conscience go on compelling us to do things in our own interest or in that of others, while it remains—this interior imperative —absolutely indifferent to what we are thinking or feeling!

There, opposing us, is the great chaotic world pressing in on all sides with its pains and pleasures; and *here,* within us, is our secret personal mind, able to think what thoughts it pleases. And yet no imperative decree of our conscience commands us to be happy in spite of all, and to cease encouraging ourselves in our unhappiness.

The odd thing is that by some weird psychological law we do derive a perverse satisfaction—not happiness but a self-pleasing sensation of malicious destruction and self-laceration—from encouraging ourselves in our black mood. It is a queer mystery, this psychology of self-pity that is the cause of so much misery in the world! It almost seems as if some evil demon in us were always hunting about for some new reason why we should feel wretched.

If it cannot find outward circumstances adapted to its purpose it rakes up other annoyances. I think sometimes we actually have a vague childish notion that we are revenging ourselves upon life and upon the universe by insisting on hugging our misery. As though the universe cared! What suffers from it is that vast invisible world of other conscious minds whose struggles with themselves make up the great tragic drama of human life. This invisible world of countless human intelligences, linked together by magnetic vibrations, receives a downward pull from the obstinate unhappiness of any single human soul.

Thus it works out that you *do* revenge yourself upon something! What one feels, however, is that it is hardly the part of a magnanimous mind to revenge itself upon the human race who are not in the least responsible, in order to punish an unsympathetic universe, or god, or fate, or evil chance, that *is* responsible.

Still more childish does it seem to go on hugging your unhappiness in order to punish some particular class in the community, some particular set of people, or even some particular person who has done you harm, when from your own showing, this class, this set of people, this particular person, cares not a jot about it! It is no punishment to *them*. If they felt anything at all about the matter they might even feel a mild satisfaction that you were unhappy. To be unhappy in order to punish! That really does seem an human instinct. But how pathetically absurd! It is like that grave, outraged, indignant look we are all in the habit of turning upon the thing when something in our path trips us up. We swing solemnly round to glare at this wrong-doing inanimate, even if it be no more than an uneven stone; and our expression at that moment has a portentous severity that is ridiculous.

It is our punishing expression, and it is to be hoped it does us good, for it is certain that the object of our wrath remains unaffected. What I mean, therefore, by "the Panergic act of the mind" is the gesture, sometimes a really heroic gesture, by which in spite of everything we insist on forcing ourselves to feel happy. What this act of the mind does is to concentrate—always with a back-consciousness that we're lucky not to be dying in extreme pain—upon a compressed essence of all the simple aspects of life that give us our chief pleasure. It is not exactly that we think to ourself, "Well! I shall at any rate be soon pulling the bed-clothes under my chin and turning over to sleep"; or that we think to ourself, "I shall soon be sitting down to a cup of tea"; or that we think to ourself "I shall soon be alone and walking along that path where there's no traffic!" or that we think to ourself, "I shall soon be getting back to my book"; or that we think to ourself, "I shall soon be talking to my girl, or to my man, over the fire", for it is rather a sensation called up by the mind than a definite thought.

But as you enjoy in your imagination a sort of thought-essence of these simple things you associate them in your mind with something sweeter, vaguer, more intangible still, with that diffused sensation of well-being which Wordsworth was thinking when he spoke of the "pleasure which there is in life itself."

I have myself sometimes experienced a most extraordinary thrill in connection with this "Panergic act" in another and further overtone. I refer to a curious sharing of your life-sensation with the life-sensation of the generations of the dead. These men of old times as they went about their affairs had just the same vague, sweet, intangible indirect sensations as we have. And over all these "little things" upon which we concentrate now, over all these small material sensations that keep alive our cosmic well-being hovers the consciousness that we are all "in the same box," all in the same familiar high-road of mischances, all between the same Inn-fire of sweet love and the same gibbet on the blasted heath.

At the bottom of everything, below love and work and beauty, and good and evil, lies this tragic alternative, this abysmal parting of the ways. Are we going to force our spirit to create the feeling of happiness within us, or are we going to yield to the demon of destruction? What, as a matter of fact, we come to feel, as we practise this Panergic gesture, is that we are doing it not only for ourselves but for *something else:* and this "something else" for which we are doing it is nothing less than the whole upward spring of the creative force in the universe.

It is not as though this happiness were an easy thing or an inevitable thing. It is not only the grand tour-de-force of our doomed mortality, it is the act by which, ere it resolves itself into the dust, *through* our mortality, strange intimations of a possible immortality reach us.

And there is a way of thinking of death from which you can get pleasure. For there is a positive something in death, just as there is in life, which has nothing to do with the pain of dying or with the decomposition of the body. No one cries out "I wish I were in pain!" but there are many people who

— 91 —

cry out "I wish I were dead!" and, when they do this, is there not an under-consciousness about it, that implies a feeling for death beyond the mere negative of the misery of life?

This mysterious positive pleasure that it is possible to associate with death quite apart from the desirability of escaping the pain of life corresponds in a measure to the delicious moment of going to sleep, which is indeed its earthly simulacrum.

Now all these primordial sensations, produced by sun and fire and food and drink and air, make up, with the sense of sleep, and with our movements between earth and sky, what might be called *the diurnal continuum* of "the pleasure which there is in life and death," and we have a right to enjoy them, as Homer so often reminds us, even at the moments of our greatest sorrows.

To turn away from the presence of tragic suffering with a burst of facetiousness—unless it were the facetiousness of a Swift or Dante, or the humour of a Shakespeare or Rabelais—would be a monstrous thing and against the grain of all natural human instinct, but to eat bread, to feel the sun, to bend over the fire, to breathe the air, to walk across the face of the earth, are sensations for which we have the plenary indulgence of Nature herself, even at our most tragic moments, as the world goes round!

For into these ancient compensations of our tragic

life death has already entered. It has touched our bread with its own terrible and magical consecration. It has entered into the flame of our hearth-fire. It has mingled with the grass we walk on, with the earth-mould into which our feet sink. It has passed into the flowing of the waters, into the substance of the sands on the shore. The taste of the bread, the breath of the air, the feeling of movement, the sense of sleep, have already become, in their long association with human life an actual part of the high invisible tragic drama in which all mental life is involved.

Daily we eat and drink and breathe our dead; nightly we are gathered to our dead in sleep. In the feelings derived from these things we become one with that great mysterious tide of Being, wherein all grief resolves itself, and which is already, since in these things the material is taken up into the immaterial, something more than mortality. With its transitory and its temporal it touches that portion of our human soul which is already outside "the body of our death."

What therefore I am struggling to describe as the Panergic act is that interior resistance of the soul, not only to misery, apathy, worry, but to the more tragic sorrows of life.

It is the basic resistance of all souls to futility and destruction, a resistance whereby we force ourselves to be happy *in spite of all,* recognizing that as long as the spirit in us is thus unconquered we are obeying the deepest imperative there is, not only the imperative of our individual conscience, but the imperative of that super-conscience of mankind as a whole that carries with it the invisible pressure of all the living and all the dead!

It seems natural enough for new-born lambs to leap and skip, but when you watch the way a human infant behaves, how long and inconsolable are its sorrows, it begins to dawn upon you that though happiness may be something to which beasts and birds are born, it is something that man—alone in this in all creation—has to win for himself by a constant effort.

Happiness for human beings *is an artificial thing.* Man has been separated from happiness in some mysterious cosmic "fall" and his whole life is a struggle to regain what he has lost.

"The Panergic act of the mind" is, according to my idea, one of the ways by which we can achieve this end. It is an inward motion of our whole being in which we gather our forces together in a magnetic resistance to that profound unhappiness which is natural to our transition-state between beast and god.

What we must aim at is a conscious fusion of all our bodily senses *in thought* rather than any definite thoughts. Mix the spirit with the senses, the god in us with the beast in us and thus grasp the pain-giving cosmos and wrestle with it! When our soul and our senses are thus fused together it is as if from the pit of our stomach, from our navel, from our organ of generation, as well as from some unifying force, deep within us, deeper down in our identity than our reason, there emerged an unconquerable power of resistance to suffering, a power that feeds upon sensation rather than upon thought, but a power that can hardly be called material, since it seems to flow *through* us from some buried nadir of life which is ours and yet more than ours.

My "Ichthian act of the mind" is a desperate leap of the soul into what for us must remain the absolute darkness of the unknown dimension that surrounds our astronomical world.

My "act of De-carnation" is a pretended projection of our centre of consciousness into the air at our side, from which detached vantage-ground it can view the limitations of our own organism and of the organisms of others.

But the "Panergic act" I am now describing is both a more natural and a more simple tool of our will to happiness than either of these. In making it we draw our consciousness and our energy out of our thought-process and concentrate them on our sensation-process.

Our spirit heaves itself up out of the depths of

our being, armoured, as it were, in our most familiar sensations, and thus armoured confronts the
pain-giving world. The sensations that seem to serve
us best at these times are our simplest reactions to
air, water, earth and fire. But every soul, thus heaving up in defiance of its worries, apathies, miseries,
will gather about it its own particular essences of
familiar feelings.

For myself I find that my feeling for the earth
under my feet, especially when it is plough-land or
grass, is my chief restoration. Second to that I would
put the feeling of firelight; and then the feeling of
sunlight. Then I would place the look of flowing
water and the feel of the blowing wind. Finally I
would name among these primary sensations,
wherein my soul armours itself as it heaves itself up,
the pleasure I get from reading a line or two of
Homer, which to me is a form of work.

This last point I want especially to emphasize, because I am sure that most human souls, when thus
turning at bay, tend to revert to their favourite
sensation of work; for in the sensation of work that
we enjoy a certain part of the weight of our human
destiny is lifted, as it is by nothing else. This "work"
may be a thing very different from looking up
words in a Lexicon. If you are a man in your garden,
it may be digging, if you are a woman it may be
sewing; but, whatever it is, it must be the thing that

in itself, apart from any ulterior purpose, gives you most of the over-tones and under-tones that belong to the "pleasure which there is in life itself."

WOMAN WITH MAN

When one is no longer "in love"—Woman's two desires—The woman's escape-world—To be kept apart from the man's—Female possessive lust—The woman's world of sensation and creation—Darby and Joan—Going beyond Darby and Joan—Woman's underlife—Happiness beyond good and evil—Don't be a perfect help-mate—The necessity of feeling desirable—Deceive him in all the spiritual essentials!

HAVING DEALT WITH THOSE ASPECTS OF THE individual's happiness that lie at the root of our separate conscious lives, I now proceed to deal with the matters that pertain to our happiness in relation to others, particularly in relation to our sex-mate.

I will try to cope first with the more difficult of the two chief tasks before me; that is to say with the tricks and devices, the arts and the habits, that I would recommend to a woman so that she may retain her individual happiness even in the trying process of living with a man.

The state of "being in love" is not only a state quite independent of affection, or pity, or tenderness, or of the reverse of these things, such as hate, cruelty, callousness; it is also independent of our own will. For a philosopher to lay down laws to lovers *as* lovers is as futile as for a king to command the tides; but no man or woman is only a lover, certainly not only a lover all the time, and many quite faithful and devoted mates are able to contemplate their man or their woman with a calm and critical detachment totally alien from that excited vision which heightens every aspect of our frail mortality.

The following remarks then are addressed to the type of woman who, though she and her mate still love each other in the sense of affection and respect, is no longer under the spell cast by that radiant condition called "being in love."

When the exalted happiness produced by that early state has faded away under the pressure of use and wont, there are liable to recur for such a woman moments of peculiar sadness and disillusionment, moments that fall upon her when the absorption of her work or the distraction of caring for her children slide for any brief period into abeyance.

Till now Nature has done everything without much aid from her own will or wisdom. Nature made her fall in love. Chance gave her a mate to love. Nature absorbed all the nervous energy she had in the bearing of her first child and in the care lavished upon it.

But all this is over now, and with or without children, with or without a job of her own, mysterious and indeed abysmal difficulties begin to heave up, threatening, and sometimes even shattering, the basis of her life's happiness.

Whence arise these troubles? Some of them of course are economic; some of them are connected with the passion of jealousy, some have to do with that sense of failure and futility that comes to so many people when the spring-tide of the senses begins to ebb and youth's idealism loses its vital resilience.

But beyond and beneath all these there is something else, something different from money-worries or physical ailments or the shattering of youthful faith, something that has to do with the stark primordial situation in which she now finds herself, she, a feminine creature, bound inexorably in bed and board to a masculine creature.

And she still wants, more than anything else, to be happy—simply to be happy! Indeed she wants this more intensely than she has ever wanted it since her childish days when she was heart-free and irresponsible.

What is wrong with her? What is wrong with her life? These are the questions that, if she has any intelligence, she keeps asking herself. Of course she is often tempted—and the more she lacks intelligence the more tempted she will be—to put the question in a different form and say to herself, and not always to herself, "What is wrong with *him?*" But the intelligent woman knows better than any philosopher can tell her that at these junctures in human life it is oneself, and not the other, who is primarily amenable to some mental change.

She turns her gaze inward therefore, not outward, and asks herself, first *what she wants* in order to feel happy with conscious awareness, as she used to feel happy under a blind obedience to Nature's tutelage; and next how to get what she wants. And it is then, I think, that she will find two separate deep desires within her, and find too, it may well be, that it is in some mysterious clash between these two desires that her happiness is perishing. She wants to assert herself, to taste to the full her feminine personality independently of her man; but she also wants to enjoy, possess, absorb into herself, and completely make her own this alien, foreign stranger to whom she is bound by a thousand invisible links of shared associations.

It will not be so necessary to insist to a woman as it would be to a man that in all these ultimate things the human soul has to go behind the normal moral code of the race and to take some of its weapons from what is called "the good" and some of its weapons from what is called "the bad." No human soul in the lonely depths of its life-struggle can afford to be meticulously exacting about the weapons it uses, or to let itself suffer from remorse when it finds itself tampering with the moral code of its race. Such a code for instance will tell it to be absolutely "honest" whereas any experience of life will make it plain that over and over again such absolute honesty is fatal, and that to preserve our secret integrity with ourselves it is often necessary to deceive others.

Why is it that, of all people, the ones who blurt out every thought that comes into their heads and every feeling they have are the ones that tend to whittle away and thin out into pallid indistinction the rich compactness of the soul within them? In the process of their impulsive self-assertion, in the indulgence of their dear honesty, they cease to want anything very deeply or intensely. The integrity of their desire dilutes itself in the witless honesty of its expression. What are called, in the particular moral code of our race at any time, "the good" and "the bad" are only rough-and-ready generalizations of old experience, and there are always arriving occasions when it is not only expedient, but advisable and necessary, to be "bad" as well as "good" in our management of life.

A woman therefore who feels that her happiness depends on the assertion of certain aspects of her personality which are independent of anything within the scope of her masculine companion has,

I feel, a deep right to make use of all her feminine craft and tact to get what her nature craves.

As Dorothy Richardson so penetratingly shows, every woman is an artist in the atmosphere she creates in her dwelling even if it be no more than a single room; and in the pursuit of this "atmosphere," created by a thousand indescribable touches, she will often find herself working with effects to which her mate is totally blind. From this instinctive labour, renewed every day, sometimes with delight and often with weariness, he will be perpetually dragging her to engage in purposes and undertakings and mental interests of his own and it will only be by a thousand repeated escapes into her own world, escapes conducted with infinite tact and cunning that she will be able to build up over his blind head and about his blunt senses the delicate fabric of her creation.

How pitiful are those ménages where the instinctive artist in the woman has been slowly murdered by the heavy-handed meddling obstinacy of the man! To be happy in the creation of this atmospheric work of art—often totally invisible to the man who inhabits it—a woman must be penetrating enough to recognise the fact that men and women are totally different in their sense-perceptions, and courageous and unscrupulous enough to go on with what she is doing without her man's knowledge or understanding.

The same thing applies to her books, her bric-àbrac, her sewing, her flowers, her little sensuous relaxations, into all of which she has a right to escape at the price of a thousand devices.

A discerning stranger will quickly detect something almost raw, crude, shocking, even indecent, about a couple's life where the woman's atmospheric cocoon-weaving—those subtle golden threads —have been frayed and torn and discoloured by the meddling of masculine obtuseness or the harsh fanaticism of masculine asceticism.

The same thing applies to her clothes. It is pure unwisdom in a woman to spoil the nature-given happiness that comes to her from the inner feeling that she "looks nice," out of a proud contempt for feminine wiles. The grating bitterness of a shrew, the dingy carelessness of a slut, are the dolorous alternatives she brings down—one or the other and not unfrequently both—upon their devoted heads by her indulgence in this intellectual whim.

The stupidest of mistakes that a woman can indulge in to spoil her happiness is not to recognise once for all that her world is totally different from her man's, and that it is waste of time to struggle and fight in a vain attempt to drag him over his boundary into hers. Her world and his are separate crystal spheres that really touch at only one point, the point of their enjoyment of each other, an enjoyment which would lose its zest if what touched were two flat boards and not a magnetic point on the curve of a living planetary circle.

The reason why you see so often such a tragic strain in the eyes of the feminine partner in a life-covenant is that this particular woman has let herself be dragged so often over the No Man's Land between their separate orbits. She has indeed ceased to revolve as an independent world with her own private feminine pleasures, and has become a dusty and bedraggled fly, clinging to the turning wheel of his taste, his peculiarities, his manias, his opinions, his conceit of himself.

But the same applies to her attempt to drag him over the line into her domain. Many men have been completely destroyed by this. Women savour deeply and mysteriously, beyond any conception of men, the general spectacle of the world. They relish with an indescribable glow, in spite of all they suffer from it, this motley procession of sights and sounds and changing human moods, as the "fitful fever" of life foams and ferments about them.

They are so much closer to Nature than men that they have the power of enjoying turbulent things and distressing things even while they are being hurt by them. This sub-aqueous pleasure of theirs in the chaotic motion of the life-stream belongs to the inmost nerves of their being; and only the wisest of them, those whose consciousness, like that of

Dorothy Richardson, can plumb this under-tide at will, are aware of the nature of their deepest happiness. But, aware of it or not, they all enjoy it, they all draw their miraculous endurance from it, they are all mediums of its occulted revelations. Every woman is a sea-shell, within whose hollow curves the great ocean of life murmurs its hidden secrets; and it is this mystic realism of theirs that evokes that indescribable smile that so often crosses their faces when they listen to man—man the abstractor of essences, man the projector of theories, man the creator of ideas, man the discoverer of laws—droning on, like a great metaphysical bumble-bee, on the high shore, "polluphloisboio thalasses," of the many-sounding deep.

As I have hinted, when an intelligent woman looks inward she finds two conflicting desires, the first driving her on to escape into her own world, that world built up out of the instincts of her body, that coral-reef world of her own hourly, daily, yearly occult creation, beneath and around whose filmy filigree-walls the wild tides of life's under-sea are forever flowing; and the second driving her on to invade the life of her man, to cover her man's body with her body, to wrap herself, "skin for skin" about her man, as a glittering boa-constrictor wraps itself about the beast it swallows, as shining phos-

phorus covers a drowning plank, or gleaming leprosy
the limbs it has doomed to die.

Upon *some* measure of satisfaction for these two
desires a woman's life-happiness depends, when the
enchanted state of being-in-love fails her and the
drugged beatitude of bearing and caring for children
has passed away or is diminished by repetition.

Let us continue then in our consideration of the
craft she must use to satisfy the first of these desires.
Of course in her real life she will often find herself
satisfying both of them together. I have watched an
elderly woman rise from her comfortable chair by
the fire and lay down her knitting in order to make
some infinitesimal change in the furniture, the china,
the drapery, the crockery, the flowers of her room.
I have seen her approach the figure of her man, as
he sits absorbed in his book, and bend over him, in
order to touch his head with her lips.

Into that light breath, into that flickering moth's
caress, there passed, as I curiously watched this
scene of "eternal recurrence," a current of electric
possessiveness so soft, so steady, so remorseless, so
implacable, so *infinite,* that my profane spirit shud-
dered to behold it, as you would shudder to behold
an animal disappearing into the distended skin, the
skin's mouth oozy with voluptuous foam, of a pos-
session-drugged python! What the man himself felt
under this man-swallowing kiss I cannot of course

be sure; but my impression was that he experienced at that moment a reaction from this particular form of "love" so intense as to amount to a nervous spasm.

Nothing causes a nastier twinge, or a more tickling itch of irritation, to the free, lonely happiness of the soul than this cannibalistic pythonish "love" when it is expressed unctuously, shamelessly, indecently, and in cold blood. It makes a person feel as if he were a final tit-bit on a plate flickered over by a well-satisfied tongue. It is a totally different matter when this possessive love is expressed fiercely, passionately, tragically. It may be dangerous at such times and even terrifying, but a sensitive person feels awe, respect, pity in its presence, not irritation, not restless rebellion, not nervous anger.

But putting aside the feelings of the man in this particular scene which I recall watching with such curious and wicked interest I have seldom beheld a human countenance more radiantly happy than that of this life-satisfied lady, as in her python's kiss she turned herself in a Shirt of Nessus that licked up to the very bone her mate's bent form. She was a happy woman then; and I think it was the contact of her rosy mouth with the ivory smoothness of her man's bald head that gave me such a funny feeling. But the real truth of the situation went much deeper.

It is the fact of a woman's "possessive love,"

though equally shameless, being so much more diffused than a man's "possessive lust," that enables
her to indulge it so much more constantly and publicly than he can indulge his. Women are very lucky
in this. Their tactile sense is so much more polymor-
phic than man's that they have the power of "feeling all over" at the least touch. Psychically they are
far less sensitive than men, as can be seen in the
way they can get beside themselves with fury, hiss
forth the most deadly things, and a few minutes
later, be as cheerful and normal as if their outburst
of furious temper, which has left their man
wounded and upset for half a day, were the merest
scud of sea-foam as the life-wave rolls on; but
their whole skin, thicker as well as softer than a
man's, is so charged with diffused erotic magnetism
that it is wonderful what deep satisfaction their
possessive love can get from the least contact of
fingers or lips.

What I wanted to cry out to that woman when
she kissed *in that way* the white skull-smooth surface of her man's head was, "For God's sake, madam,
wait till you are in bed!" But to have expressed
even by a glance that gross, ribald, caddish, bawdy,
lecherous, brutal masculine thought would have been
unpardonably unkind to this excellent woman, who
was after all only letting herself be at that moment
supremely happy in the shameless indulgence of

her heart's desire. It "amuses me," as the spiteful ladies say when they mean "I get wicked pleasure," when the same women who find the Rabelaisian element in a man's books unpleasantly indecent indulge in public orgies of possessive love. What they really feel—because of the magnetic conductorship of their lively skins—is just as "indecent" as anything that a man does; in other words it is a normal, natural inevitable feeling, and one that, like the satisfaction of all innocent lust, is a legitimate part of the fulfilment of human happiness; but my lady must forgive me if I retain my view that this particular sensual basis of our happiness gains rather than loses by a certain proud and crafty secrecy.

But what finally impressed me, as I peered so curiously at this harmless scene out of the hollow slits in my Paleolithic skull, was that when my good woman finally returned to her chair and resumed her knitting a look of beatitude even beyond the radiance evoked by that sensual kiss took possession of her and I recognized that her eyes as they casually lifted from her needles rested on that little alteration she had made among the flower-vases on the mantel-shelf, which was her last touch to her coral "pleasure-dome" built in the depths of the fabulous Gulf-stream of life; and what entered my prying head was that the happiness she got when her man was relegated to the background of her life—I don't mean separated from her even for a day but back-grounded into agreeable harmlessness—was a happiness more enjoyable as well as more desirable than the sensation that gave her that look of tipsy delight as she kissed the ivory-white skull.

But she couldn't have had those lovely feelings and she couldn't have floated in such exquisite contentment on the mere flowing of the life-stream, without asking for anything, without thinking of past or future, if it had not been for the presence in the background of that egg-smooth ivory-polished cranium. Oh, how often I have watched women by themselves and women with their men and noted the different psychic "tempo" of their moods in those two conditions! My private conclusion has been that the path to happiness for a woman lies in making her man comfortable in his background, and then leaving him alone there, while she enjoys herself in her own way and after her own secretive humming-bird-moth fashion, either in her thoughts and feelings while she works and ponders on alterations in her room, or as she drifts down the street, past the shop-windows or through the booths of the Fair, pondering on alterations in the adornment of her own person.

Escape, escape, escape! That is what every woman should aim at. Escape from her man, from her children, from her friends, and above all from her parents. Not necessarily by running away—though she always has that as a last resource—but escape by a thousand crafty wiles of her mother-wit. The enchanted state of being-in-love is in itself a super-escape, but one in which both she and her lover are lifted up by Nature into a world where, while it lasts, the woman's desire and the man's desire find identical fulfilment.

Into this earthly paradise it is hard to enter again, when the pressure of common life and custom and recurrence have once closed those magic gates. Faint glimpses of it a woman gets now and again, more often I think than does her mate; but it is only when by reason of their catching together some gleam of the mystic light, cast brokenly for a second on some object, some idea, some fancy, and moving them equally and simultaneously, they are caught out of themselves, that there is a real mutual revisiting of that lost Eden.

When I experienced that curious shock, as of something indecent, by seeing that woman I spoke of just now kissing with the calm kiss of possessive sensuality her partner's polished skull I certainly did not feel any breath of Eden in what I saw; and why not? Because that caress proceeded from what in a woman corresponds to dispassionate lust in a man. It was a *kiss from the demesne below the waist,*

a kiss unshared, a reducing kiss. Many maternal
kisses are of this kind, as children know too well,
and what they really do, such kisses, is to reduce
and bring low the object which is their prey. There
is a tinge of something akin to a placid sub-sadism
in such kisses. To the deadly eye of a really penetrating clairvoyance there appears a vision of the
victim of them growing palpably smaller and smaller
beneath them, until he dwindles into helpless and
idiotic babyhood.

I am of course thinking now of the effect upon
the man's happiness of this indulgence in possessive
lust by his woman; but it still remains that if a
woman is to be happy in her life there must be
found place and scope for this kind of thing. It
goes too deep with her to be left in abeyance. The
truth is that between a man and a woman when
their state of being-in-love no longer lifts them out
of themselves into that magic mutual world created
by the super-senses of the ideal man-woman, there
must be, if they are both to be happy, a fair and
equal exchange of patient passivity. The woman,
who no longer responds to the man's lust as they
lie side by side, must be wise and generous to feelings beyond her reach, while the man must, in
justice to her, be equally prepared to feel himself
dwindling into a preposterous babyhood under her
pseudo-maternity. It is only in the state of being-

in-love that both the male-lust and the female-lust
are caught up, transported, illuminated, spiritual-
ized, identified, unified, but this does not mean,
when a couple are kind to each other, that their
basic desires must go unsatisfied.

But the first fulfilment of a woman's secret desire, when use-and-wont have blunted the passion
of love and turned it into affection and tenderness,
must always lie in one grand escape, an escape into
her own separate individual world, a world into
which it is a grievous mistake, and one attended
by inevitable unhappiness, to try to drag her mate
and her offspring. This is indeed a thing that a
true feminine instinct will always warn her from
attempting; but it is a thing for which she has a
beautiful substitute. Every woman carries about with
her her own inviolably precious world, but if certain of the fabrics out of which it is woven are
the reduced-to-babyhood or the reduced-to-doll-
hood state of her children and their father, the deli-
cacy and subtlety of her art will consist in the fact
that these living fabrics of her airy creation are
totally unconscious of what is done with them and
made of them.

The question, "What is she doing all this time,
while we are at work and at play?" is a question
that must often in a dumb, blind fashion cross the

minds of her offspring and her mate. And what *is* she doing? Well! She is escaping into her own world of sensation and creation, a world that links her girlhood with her womanhood, a world which all other women, save her own daughters, can make shiver to its foundations, but to which no man from the beginning of history has the faintest clue!

The unhappy women in our world are not the poor, the sick, the unadmired, the unappreciated. They are the ones who have not acquired the art to be the creators of a concrete yet infinite atmosphere. Worries and cares are the lot of all, and most women bear their marks on their faces; but who has not been astonished, as if in the presence of a miracle, by the well-spring of happiness that radiates from below these anxiety-scars and these sorrow-scars in the faces of even the most calamitous?

These are they who make use of their nearness to Nature, make use of their immersion in Reality, make use of their gusto for the Drama of Life, to create an atmospheric crystal-globe about them wherein they can live and move independently of chance and fate and destiny.

It were irrelevant in a discussion of human happiness to say more of the too quickly passing state of being-in-love than that by fusing together as it does the diverse sense-reactions and imaginative response to life of the male and female a super-vision of things is attained which in its richness and strangeness surpasses all other felicity.

What men and women have separately to do when first love is gone is to recover in stray flashes and glimpses that heightened vision of the world which can never come again. It came because of the fusion of the man's response to the life-stream with the woman's; and their subsequent life is an attempt to reach on their different paths this lost vision. I say on their *different* paths; for many couples make themselves bitterly unhappy by obstinately struggling to go on seeing the world as a unit when the time of this is past. What happens when they go on struggling for this against the flow of the life-tide is that they are only able to unite on a lower plane, a plane which, instead of lifting their natures up to a more thrilling happiness, is forever bringing it down to a level of the ordinary and the normal that neither of their souls if left to itself could endure for a moment.

And they bank up each other in this narrow and limited vision until any outside soul approaching them soon recognizes the hopelessness of persuading either of them to break new and original ground. By slow degrees their two independent spirits have come to this lamentable pass, that they prefer comfort to adventure, and unillumined security to the dangerous excitement of mental growth.

Even when this does not happen there is a danger of their propping each other up in all manner of unworthy and narrow prejudices, prejudices and mental limitations, that, if they had not been protected and defended, each by the other, could never have resisted the wholesome shocks and violences of circumstance.

The kind of human happiness I am concerned with in this book is, as I have tried to indicate, something more than the mere resisting of disagreeable shocks, it is a growing and a positive thing with a quality of intensity; and it is this quality of intensity so deeply charged with vital force when the two magnetic sex-poles were functioning together as a unit under the spell of the state of being-in-love that must now be won again in the separate secret life of each individual soul. The living together of two souls no longer fused by the fire of their first passion is a serious menace to any exalted happiness; but on the other hand the mere resistance to this danger, if both the man and the woman rise to the occasion, has in it potentialities of a subtle tension, out of which a richer measure of happiness can be attained by both of them, than would be possible had they missed this associated experience.

The "escape" of each of them into a deeper, an intenser level of individual life is now the goal, but who can escape if there is nothing to escape from? And compared with the "jumping-off-ground" of this intimate relation between two souls, thus inextricably bound together, the irresponsible ups and downs of casual light-of-loves offer nothing solid enough to be an effective *point d'appui* for any integrated human happiness.

One of the most interesting and complicated of all possible psychological situations arises in the case of men and women who still go on living together, bound by a thousand emotional and economic ties when the glamour of passionate love has faded. When there is no deep temperamental clash—or even when there *is,* and custom and self-control has bridged it over—such a couple may grow so close together as actually to come to resemble each other in certain physical ways. Sharing day by day endless little pre-occupations, endless little hardships and reliefs, there is evoked on the surface of their two natures an identical crust of resistance to discomfort, an identical "sensitive plate" of enjoyment of comfort, which at once grows more opaque as against the outer world, and sinks down deeper into the yielding substance of their separate beings, as their association continues. To the casual stranger crossing their path, these Darbys and Joans, these Williams and Margarets, and Johns and Jennies, seem like two branches of

the same tree, two heads of the same dragon, two
flames of the same hearth, two clock-figures of the
same automatic time-piece and their associated identity produces in such a stranger a peculiar and special sense of pleasure, a pleasure which draws its
poignance from all the obstacles to such an adjust-
ment that he has experienced in his own life and
from that curious satisfaction, half-moral and half-
aesthetic, that even the most wilful and inartistic
person derives when some immemorial human
yearning, like the yearning after an ideal unity
between men and women, has apparently, in one
case at least, been fulfilled.

But genuine and deep though this mysterious
human pleasure may be in the contemplation of
our well-mated John and Joan, there are, for any
searching and exacting mind, many serious after-
thoughts with regard to the spiritual quality of this
peaceful and comfortable association. It is a marriage of kindred feelings, of kindred enjoyments,
it is a marriage that has evoked a common "sensitive
plate" of little comforts and securities, but, for all
that, a real philosopher of happiness will hesitate
to pronounce it a "marriage of true minds."

The penetrating Dutch novelist, Couperus, has
gone so far as to pillory one couple of this type in
the complacent and self-indulgent figures of Karel
and Kateau, a couple who certainly relish the par-

ticular "happiness" they have reached by converting their private selfishness into a double-charged unit of common selfishness, but whose "happiness" is lacking in all elements of imagination, intellect, or spirit.

And there is always a danger that this superficial encrustation of mutual sensual enjoyment, when all shocks or disturbing vibrations from the outer world are muffled and padded away, shall grow into something most deadly and destructive to all the more thrilling and exultant inspirations. Any adequate art of happiness keeps its eye upon quality as well as upon quantity, and balances the positive thrilling moments against the merely negative avoidance of discomfort and annoyance. The danger of this common encrustation of a united response to small sensual comforts is that it can so often only be attained by both the parties giving up what is most characteristic and spirited and illuminating in their different sexes. The subtlest instincts of a woman's soul are not the same as the subtlest instincts of a man's soul, and yet here they both are converting the proud and obstinate questionings of two mysterious living souls into perpetual fussing about keeping out draughts, winding their clocks, cossetting their digestions, trimming their lamps, mixing their drinks, dealing their cards, while the wind in the chimney is calling to her, and the rain on the window is calling to him, in wild, intermittent, desperate reminders that the cosmic mystery which men call happiness is not to be gained by a conspiracy of clinging bodies, but by the fraternization of proud and lonely intelligences.

The real deep reward of any life *à deux* is not gained by toning down the eternal *woman* in her and the eternal *man* in him to a sub-human skill in avoiding draughts and damp and rats and indigestion and economic worry and a sub-human fastidiousness in the pleasures of the table, but by both of them carrying the high, proud, subtle, separate peculiarities of their sex to the most exultant limit. Let Jack Sprat and his wife "lick their platter clean," there is a spiritual "fat" and a spiritual "lean" in the stream of life adapted to far greater differences between the two than these felicitous divergencies of palate.

As a matter of fact an intelligent stranger will often detect in these "happy" marriages, where, apparently, two selfishnesses have become one selfishness, that the whole thing is a successful masquerade. It is not, and never was, *two* selfishnesses! It is one selfishness; but a selfishness so crafty as to have the power, like certain low forms of marine life, of splitting itself into two, and incarnating this second self in the body of the partner of its life.

What makes the test of a really happy partnership

between a man and a woman, a partnership with the full creative flow of Nature's "intention" behind it, is the retention by each of them of the full flavour, not only of their separate sex-peculiarities, but of their separate personal peculiarities. The more different they are and the more different they remain the better!

How can such a delicate thing, such an intricately built-up thing and such an *artificial* thing, as the happiness of intelligent persons in this tragic world, afford to neglect the great natural up-welling of magnetic vitality that comes when a woman gives herself to being a woman and a man gives himself up to being a man? To neglect the power of sex in any question of this sort is like trying to make bricks without straw.

To return therefore to those two profound feminine desires which, if even partially satisfied, make a woman happy, as we have already hinted the satisfaction of the first of these has to do with her own secret life as an individual feminine person totally apart from both her mate and her offspring, while the second has to do with her devouring and swallowing up, like an insanely possessive python, both her offspring and her mate.

Now it must be understood once and for all that the roots of every individual's happiness descend be-

low the level of life where what we call good and
evil begin to differentiate themselves. So that to say
that a woman *ought not* to have these possessive
feelings is as absurd as to say that water ought not
to flow, or fire burn, or ice freeze.

The whole point is, how is she going to control
these feelings of possessiveness, this desire to absorb
those she loves into the substance of her flesh, so
that it should be the cause of intense happiness to
herself, and not unpleasant, to her mate and her
children? Fortunately, by the compensatory law of
balance in these matters, her man too, *as* a man,
has a profound desire of his own which is quite as
"wicked" and rooted quite as deep in that sub-
stratum below the dividing line of good and evil,
as is her all-swallowing love.

I refer to his impersonal masculine lust. This
impersonal lust, for all its familiar association with
one feminine body, remains as non-human, as un-
tender, as uncivilized, as satyrish and paleolithic, as
it often became—sometimes to her astonishment—in
the first days of their love-making.

Not far from where I write these lines in an
ancient walled town where Caesar's legionaries wor-
shipped Venus, there stands, for all to see, the
phallic image of what is called the Cerne Giant.
Now there is a "Cerne Giant" in every man, and a
"Cerne Giant" quite as wicked in *his* way as the

all-swallowing Python in every woman is wicked in *hers,* a "Cerne Giant" who wants to make love to his woman *as if to a strange woman,* as if to *any* woman, as if to *womanhood in the abstract,* as if to the de-personalized essence of femininity, temporally in-carnated in the familiar body at his side, and a "Cerne Giant" too who, if he had not learned in his long life-history a certain moderation, would be as destructive, on his side, to the object of his attraction as the Python in woman might be to the object of hers.

It was the purring hiss of this Lamia-Demon in every woman that I must have been conscious of, when I shrank away in disgust from those clinging lips pressed against that ivory-white skull; but woe to the man who ever dares to show irritation when his woman suddenly kisses him.

"When women kiss" might be the title of a very profound novel, and no doubt there are a thousand aspects to this psychological problem, but reverting to that particular case and to many other parallel ones, it has gradually become clear to me that what fills a woman with a sudden irresistible desire to kiss her man is neither admiration nor pity. It is an over-powering thrill at seeing his dignity, his self-possession, his powerfulness, his masterfulness, his self-importance, brought down and the man's unfledged, unfrocked, undefended, un-armoured, naked identity *exposed.*

She kisses him with a sudden spasm of melting tenderness when she sees him grown small, grown helpless, grown naked, ready to be rocked and lulled and comforted and fed, at her breast and on her lap.

So often must she have kissed with just such a sudden spasm of tenderness an angry and screaming infant, that a faint tinge of diffused sadism clings about this kiss of hers, the immemorial Python kiss, with which she gathers her coils, like those of the mythological world-snake, about the foolish idol of her deep heart, reduced to something stripped, helpless, exposed, but at the same time to something *by no means contemptible.*

I know I am fumbling towards a very deep mystery in this; but I believe that what attracts a woman so irresistibly at such moments is not at all an unworthy or ignoble aspect of her man. It may be the diffused sadism of the doll-loving maternalism in her nerves that is her dominant urge but the uncompromising realism of her sex has much to do with it too. I think it is always at the moments when her man is most unconscious of himself, most disarmed of what you might call his masculine philosophical detachment that she feels this wave of irresistible emotion, this stir of a feeling in her which corresponds, on the feminine plane, to what in men is called lust.

It is when he is absorbed rather in what he is doing than in what he is feeling or thinking, so that his essential identity, stripped of all mental over-tones, stripped of all pride, vanity and conceit, is *caught off-guard*, without mask or sword or wig, and found to resemble a touchingly pre-occupied animal lost in its immediate business, that his woman thus leaps upon him with her irresistible python-kiss. While she is in the state of being-in-love she gets her thrill of happiness from idealizing her man, but when her "being-in-love" has changed to "loving" this idealizing ceases and its place is taken by what would seem to the man, if he only knew about it, a pitiless and terrible realism. But this is the nature of "love" in a woman; that love which not only outlasts "being-in-love" but outlasts the most savage and deadly quarrels. For it seems that when women love at all they love a man's inalienable self, that self which his dignity, his pride, his masterfulness, his grandiose gestures, as well as his lust and his weakness, conceal, and conceal too not only from the world but from himself. This is the self in him that his woman loves when she has ceased to be in love and sometimes *before she has ceased to be in love,* and although it is a self that lacks all intellectual grandeur and all picturesque charm, though it is, in a sense, a stripped, reduced and exposed self, it is not a contemptible self, for after all it is the self of a man, a unique living man, "among such as eat bread upon the earth."

Little girls do exactly this very thing with the doll they love best, a doll that indeed often looks, when a stranger sets eyes on it, as if it had very little beauty left. There is as a matter of fact a kind of outrage, a kind of impiety and sacrilege, when a man-thinker attempts as I am attempting now, to indicate the tricks and devices by which a woman can be happy. A woman's happiness is rarely a mental thing, rarely a self-conscious thing. It is so close to the ebb and flow of Nature's most intimate tides that it is a thing much more difficult to make subject to the rational will or even to the imaginative reason than the happiness of a man.

It is indeed, at its deepest and most natural, just that very "pleasure which there is in life itself" of which Wordsworth speaks, who for all his formalities and pedantries got closer to the essential life of young girls and to the essential life of girl-mothers, than any other writer. The one generalization about feminine happiness that I do feel safe in registering, is that, whatever it is, it is neither made nor marred by the changes that take place in morals, in attire, or even in the fashions of the toilet. A woman sticking faithfully to one love, a woman rushing about between a dozen loves, a woman with short skirts, a woman with long skirts, a woman with her eyelashes and eyelids and lips and cheeks and tresses left as Nature made them, a woman with these mortal appendages transformed out of all recognition, has the same deep sensational under-life of happiness or unhappiness. Some old-fashioned women are happy, others deeply unhappy. Some modern girls are nervous wrecks; others are sane, practical and sturdy, and full of lively joy.

Many good women are perfectly miserable, many "bad" women are radiantly content. So that all a philosophical adviser of these strange Beings can do, Beings between whose mysterious knees the human generations are born and die, is to offer to their consideration certain mental tricks and turns and attitudes such as might conduce to their secret happiness whether they decide to run away from their husbands, or to stay with their husbands, whether they decide to take a couple of new lovers or to renounce all lovers, whether they decide to cut off their hair and paint their lips and pluck out their eyebrows or to preserve their "innocence" *à la* Greuze, or their dignity *à la* Raphael.

Some masculine philosophers express the view that there is something delicate and tender and vir-ginal, a sort of imponderable vegetative bloom and magical quietness about the natural state of women which is preserved better by the old-fashioned fidelity to one hulking fool rather than by the new-fangled picking and choosing between a score of hulking fools, but the luck or ill-luck in this alterna-tive depends so much upon individual peculiarities that it seems very rash to dogmatize about it.

It is true that the new liberty has made many young women profoundly unhappy. You see on many faces a hunted, harassed, reckless, lacerated, forced gaiety, as lamentable as the endearments of a worn-out whore; but it is better to be reckless and alive than resigned and dead, and this modern lacerated look, wherein the virginal bloom of a woman's instinctive charm has been harrowed by a thousand plough-shares, is nothing to the despairing, "tied-to-the-stake" expression of so many old-fashioned wives.

But as I am trying so hard to make clear, first from one point of view and then from another, the best way for a woman to be happy is to let her whole nature flow like water—in spite of all obstacles and defiance of all moral codes—along the two main channels of her instinctive heart's desire. This desire—and I am sure most women will agree with me in this—is to have what is called "a life of her own," a life in which she can escape into herself and into her most secret personal sensations and also seize upon, and possess, and flow round and about, and enjoy as a little girl enjoys a funny-looking battered doll, some skipping male whose personality she has idealized at first sight, and is therefore condemned to contemplate forever and to subject forever to all her furies and execrations, in his stripped essence of unadorned reality.

Yes, for a man to be made happy, the desirable situation is comparatively simple. He wants his pride satisfied, his lust satisfied, his conscience satisfied, his love of work and his love of play satisfied.

But making a woman happy is a much more complicated business. Conscience has nothing to do with it, pride very little, lust hardly anything, and neither work in the ordinary sense nor play in the ordinary sense, emerge as of primary importance. She must have scope *to live to herself* which means the building up out of herself and the house she lives in of a subtle and highly "stylized" work of art, a work of art which surrounds her like a mother-of-pearl shell, and is the projection in material form of her essential soul; and she must also be so treated by her man that she has peace and quiet enough in his company to reduce her ideal of him to a reality, and yet to a reality which, for all its unconscious helplessness, is full of the touching pathos of simple human integrity. She will be wise, it seems to me, to go to work in both these pursuits with a complete indifference to considerations of good and evil.

I would like this little work to be a Devil's Hand-Book for young women, or if you prefer, a Machiavel's Breviary on the topic of "How to be happy without having to be good," for it seems harder for most of the people I encounter to escape

the unfair demands made upon them by their consciences than to resist monstrous and inhuman temp-
tations. Most of the people whose paths I cross are
perpetually being ordered by their conscience to put
up at all costs with what makes them unhappy.
What I am aiming at as the Devil's advocate in this
book is to persuade their consciences that they owe
it to the mystery of the universe and to the mystery
of life to be happy at all costs, *if possible without
running away,* but at any rate to be happy.

Nor need any woman exact of her man that he
should notice the nice touches she puts to her house
and to her person. Short of robbing him of food
and fire and tobacco, short of getting him into debt,
it is "very meet and right" as the prayer-book says,
that she should spend his money on this wonderful
private work of art; but she must do it *for herself
alone.* A man pays for it. That is enough. In pay-
ing for it he pays for the privilege of not having
to notice it.

Of course when the pair are still in the exalted
state of being-in-love everything that the woman
has touched becomes an enchanted mystery to the
man; but even in these days she, much more than
he, continues living her own life and seeing things
in her own realistic way totally independent of her
lover's fervent imagination.

But now that their mystical attempt to respond to

— 131 —

the universe as one unit is at an end, now that they are—what it is not less interesting to be—a man enjoying himself in *his* way and a woman enjoying herself in *her* way, if she wants to be happy she must be quite unscrupulous about escaping into herself. The more she escapes into herself the better for both of them and it is much easier to do it with only her mate and her children at her side than to do it with her mother at her side! A mother has far more power over a daughter than over a son, and almost always an evil power, a power that most subtly reduces a daughter's happiness. The mother does not *wish* to do this, but it is clear enough that if you have two creators of the same work of art under the same roof one of the two will have no occupation; and this one naturally will be the younger.

A girl is happier living with almost any man who does not get drunk and beat her than with the best of mothers. There is a deep and sinister mystery about the relation between a mother and daughter. One feels as if there were something evil, some subtle outrage to nature, about their living together at all. A girl would be always wise to choose to live next door to her man's mother rather than under the same roof with her own, for it is better to quarrel openly and flagrantly than to be covertly and unconsciously vampirized at the very root of your identity. The mother gave. The mother taketh away. But both in this giving and this taking what is good for a son, adding to his egoism and detracting from his egoism, is deadly and fatal to a girl. The only good mothers are for girls are the mothers who have the power of *letting go their hold*.

The way for a woman to be happy is to enjoy her identity as a woman to the extremest limit. Let her derive all the most subtle sensations she can from her room, from her house, from her own body and from what she wears. Let her read, not what she feels she *ought* to read but what she enjoys reading. Let her live boldly for all those little things that really thrill her; for her fabrics, her garden, her window-plants, her curtains, her china, her favorite actors, comedians, musicians, preachers.

Let her make a great deal of the view from her windows, especially from her kitchen window. If she cannot enjoy these little pleasures openly and easily let her enjoy them surreptitiously, evasively, indirectly. Her life is *her* life, not her man's, just as his life is *his* and not hers. It is one of the ultimate secrets of happiness for a man and woman who want to go on living together when the early romance of their passion has been modified by habit that they should drastically give up the attempt to share all their pleasures. They will only lose one thing to gain another thing; and this new thing that they will gain will be ten thousand times more evocative of happiness than the attempt to feel in cold-blood, when they have fallen back into their separate identities, the old united sensations, which, as far as the woman was concerned, were never quite as fused as the good simple male lover imagined them to be.

She is a woman. He is a man. They are not, they never can really be, "one flesh," still less one soul. Nothing is so deadly to a woman's real natural secret happiness—except life with her mother—than a devoted attempt to become the perfect help-mate. Why should she become the help-mate rather than he? His work, his life, his sensations are those of a man; hers those of a woman. At many points they naturally meet, and their achievements then have all the greater power because they bring to bear on those critical issues the combined magnetic force of two separate parallel streams.

What interferes with a woman's happiness more than anything else is the constant pressure of two sets of worries, her own and her man's. He, if he be wise, is always escaping into his own world. Let her do the same. Let her humour him, flatter him, encourage him, console him; but there is one thing she must never sacrifice to him, her private secret enjoyment of her own feminine sensations.

As a matter of fact she lives much nearer to

Nature than he does. The thousand and one moods of weather, the effects of daylight, of firelight, of lamp-light, of cold and heat, of the expressive shapes, groupings, atmospheres, colours and forms of the inanimate world of *things,* evoke hourly responses in her to which he is totally oblivious.

Let her never be betrayed into growing callous and indifferent to all these delicate appeals of atmosphere, to all these fitful beckonings of forms and colours, to all these wavering impressions of air and light that make up a woman's deepest awareness. Whatever her worries and his worries may be, let her make it a point of aesthetic conscience to drive them all away at certain moments and to force her troubled mind into harmony with her relaxed senses. She will then, as she gives way to some "blessed mood" over her sewing, over her book, over whatever it may be in her mechanical house-work that allows her a kind of half leisure, find herself thrilled by the obscure stirring within her of all those vague marginal feelings that compose the sub-tide of her feminine life.

But if she claims the right to escape, however furtively, into these passing essences of her especial inanimate world, she must on her side be indulgent to *his* escape from their common worries into *his* private little pleasures. And she must remember that chief among these pleasures is his attraction to her own body. Towards these feelings of his however reluctant she may be, a wise and generous woman—so long as the birth-control problem has been settled—would not wish to be anything but docile and kind, remembering that what is called "lust" in a man has its parallel in those more diffused but probably no less sensual feelings which come over her sometimes with such a rush when she catches his essential identity so stripped, so disarmed, so "boyish" in his moments of pre-occupied absorption.

But it cannot be insisted upon too often that for a woman to be happy when the glamour of being-in-love has ebbed it is above all things necessary for her to be spiritually independent and emotionally self-sufficient. This self-sufficiency, however, does not at all mean that she ceases to think about her body or about the pleasure-giving power of her body. The pleasurable feeling that she "looks nice" is a pleasure primarily for herself alone. The feeling that her body is a desirable body, a body provocative, wherever she carries it, to the sensuality of men, is a *secondary* consideration. A woman subtle in the art of happiness makes the utmost of all the "narcissism," all the self-love, she can possibly summon up. This is the deepest secret of all. To be profoundly happy according to Nature's intention, a woman has to feel—how shall I put it?

—as if the furniture of her room were in love with her, as if all the walls and floors were enamoured of her, as if the very candle on her table "bowed towards her," as the poet says, to "under-peep her eyelids"; she has to feel as if the sunlight on her window-sill were her lover, as if the rain on the roof were her suitor, as if the wind in the chimney were sighing to caress her; she has to feel as if the impalpable pulse of the solid earth outside, the imponderable pressure of the divine ether above, were both drawn in a delicious confederacy of planetary attraction towards their daughter and their darling.

What she must get into her head is—and let her pretend it if she doesn't believe it!—that every woman in the world has something *physically desirable* about her. As a matter of fact there would be no "pretence" about it, if it were not for that self-lacerating demon in the heart of an unhappy woman who refuses to leave her the least semblance of desirability.

But ask Papa Karamazov about this, he who found that poor deformed village-idiot, the mother of Smerdyakov, so sweet a morsel for his wicked joy. Papa Karamazov found in fact *something desirable* about every woman in the world. It was his grand discovery, and for all his rascality it made him a happy man.

It is sheer madness and morbidity in any woman,

however plain, not to give herself the thrill of feeling that she is desirable—and desirable for her body too; for the women who try to base their secret happiness on their mental gifts neither understand Nature or themselves. Let a woman cultivate her mental gifts by all means, but when it comes to this delicious, imponderable, inexpressible happiness, which—in spite of all her worries, and all her man's worries, and all the burden of their offspring—is for her "the pleasure which there is in life itself" it is her body that must give it to her, not her mind.

There is a "Papa Karamazov" in the earth, in the sun, in the air, in the walls of her house, in her garden; there is a "Papa Karamazov" in the Creator who made her, in the Evolutionary Mystery that desires to use her for its purpose, as well as, actually or potentially, in the personality of every man she meets.

A woman who has any skill at all in the art of happiness will keep enough independence of mind, and enough consciousness of the desirability of her body, *to remain her man's mistress* in spite of the fact that she is bearing his children.

But this deep consciousness of the desirability of her body—however poorly clothed and overworked and undernourished—must not be confined to being her man's mistress. She must feel desirable with every man she meets—and not only with every man! I touch here upon a secret of life that the psychoanalysts have completely neglected. I mean the particular kind of attraction that women, who are not Lesbians at all, feel for each other. To be happy with that deep, fluid, pervasive, I might almost say *chemical* happiness, that is only waiting to brim over from the Sacred Fount and invade every nerve and fibre, a woman ought to feel her desirability first with regard to the elements, that is to say with regard to the Cosmos, then with regard to herself, then with regard to other women, then with regard to her particular man.

However harassed and poor and haggard and ill-dressed any woman may be no day should pass without her letting herself love herself and feel soft and delicious and lovely *for* herself. She may be mending stockings, washing at the sink, digging in the garden, baking bread in the oven, suckling her child, lighting the fire, laying the table, but if she has not allowed all the magic of life to drain away from her by misuse and abuse, she ought to be able to yield herself up to that mysterious embrace of the universe, in which she feels that she loves everything in the world and is loved by everything in the world. Those extraordinary feelings of rapturous happiness that come sometimes to women, when, thinking of "something else," they suddenly see their whole life in a new perspective and feel as if it were over-poweringly lovely, have to do, not with her mind at all, but with an elemental reciprocity that exists between life itself and the feminine senses.

And let her extend this voluptuous secret life of the senses, wherein she loves herself and feels her-self loved by inanimate things, into all her human encounters, whether with men or women. Every woman ought to be a bride of the universe in that same mystic sense with which nuns—who with all they renounce never renounce their essential femininity—are brides of the Mystery behind the universe; and this mystical radiance, this emanation of magical happiness that she draws from life—and in a sense from death too, for every woman is a Persephone caught up between life and death—she ought to have the power of transmitting in the subtle chthonian smile with which she greets every-one who approaches her.

A woman who understands the art of arts, the art of being a woman, will never have need to cuckold her mate with any particular man. There is not a human being who looks her in the face to whom she does not give a life-restoring drop from the sacred fount, to whom in a psychic sense she does not offer herself. She offers herself in her smile. She offers herself in her expression. She offers herself with every movement and with every rest from movement.

And what above all this woman offers, this woman who has learnt the oldest of all arts, the art subtler than literature, more magical than poetry, the art the lack of which in the Creator of our cosmos "brought death into the world and all our woe, with loss of Eden," is the gift of being happy after past tragedy, with the possibility of future tragedy, and while tragedy is going on around.

This is that Nepenthe that Helen of Troy brought back from Egypt. This is also that morsel of Pomegranate tasted by Persephone in the Kingdom of Dis.

For the ultimate meaning of that feminine smile that bewildered Homer, maddened Dante, and tantalised Leonardo, that smile of a woman who apparently understands what men do not understand, has to do with death as well as life; and whatever else it is, it not only takes something from life and appropriates it to death, but takes something from death and appropriates it to life. It is hard to tell what women are thinking of when they smile this particular smile, this smile of Persephone, but they certainly are not thinking of unhappiness, though *something* tragic, that does not at the same time imply misery or despair, is not far off.

Whatever this mystic-tragic but not unhappy

smile may be that seems to express the secretest depth of women's happiness in life and possibly her sense of "the pleasure which there is in life and death," it is clear that men have no form of expression corresponding to it; and its isolated existence seems to be a yet further proof that the way to be happy for a woman living with a man is to live to herself, to the universe, to God, and only now and again cling to her mate with her pythoness kiss. This proud spiritual isolation—which I am certain is the only way for a couple to live happily together when they are no longer in love—does not mean that they don't contemplate each other's lives with humorous, tender, and infinitely indulgent relish.

I am revealing one of the basic paradoxes and contradictions at the root of life; but the truth is that the more deeply a woman lives to herself and retreats into her own world of sensations the more generous and indulgent she can be to her man and the happier she can make him. It is the petulant, jealous and corroding strain of trying to trail after him and cling to him when he debouches into *his* secret world that gives her the unhappy look you see on so many women's faces. Let her find her pride satisfied in each separate moment that she can snatch from the passing of time, as she sits sewing at her window, or by her fire, with her book on her lap,

with the vague sensuousness of the mysterious well-
being of a woman at rest buoying her up, like a
calmly-rocking wave in an infinite sea.

The great thing to avoid is the blurting out of
her terrible woman's insight into her man's weaknesses. Deceive him, deceive him, deceive him in
all the great spiritual essentials but be honest about
the little things; above all about money. In the
greater things duplicity is the word. By this I mean
never let him guess how far you see round him, how
deep you see through him, and how disillusioned
you are with regard to his pathetic masculine conceit. Such "duplicity" in reality—such is the irony
of life—comes much nearer the truth than any
angry outbursts you might make in merciless con-
demnation of his weaknesses. You are nearer to
Nature than he is. Nature is feminine, just as you
are, and is forever whispering her secrets into your
ear. You must remember that it is men and not
women who invented language, who invented the
words you have to use, words that as soon as you
utter them distort your feminine meaning. Your
flattery of him, your humouring of him, your constant spiritual deception of him is the price he has
to pay for wanting to live with a being of a different race, and then insisting that this being should
talk to him in *his* tongue rather than her own.

There is no need for you, either, to unburden yourself to another woman, still less to betray him to another man. Sink deep down into your own soul, and analyse not your love. Live in your own sensations. All women belong to a race far older than the race of man, and a race who have known for thousands of years what he is only beginning now to articulate with his blundering reason.

To argue with him is pure insanity. Humour him, agree with him, and think your own thoughts! It is only a desperately foolish woman, and one devoid of all pride, who goes chattering to other women about her man. Satisfy your superiority, not in trying to prove to him that you are cleverer than he is, but in seeing how far you can go in concealing from him your deeper insight. Nature has made you "loving" enough. Nature will deal with the continuance of your "love." Learn from Nature another lesson, a more difficult lesson. Learn to live a double life; *the life with him,* which, if you have any penetration, must be a life of a thousand spiritual deceptions, *and the life with yourself,* to which in the nature of things he has no clue.

Let him go on thinking in his folly that you love him for his intellect, for his character, for his strength, for his humour, for his imagination, for his good looks. What you really love him for it is wisest never to reveal to him. Nature and yourself know what it is, that stripped, pre-occupied, heart-breakingly simple man-doll, whom you catch off-guard sometimes, nearly giving yourself away to him by the poignance of what you feel. But you must not give yourself away; for what he wants, unless he happens to have more of the woman in his own soul than is usual with his tribe, is not just to be loved, least of all just to be loved for his pathetic, reduced, poignant, tragic-comic identity, but to be loved with wonder and awe and reverence and admiration, feelings that come easily to you in the initial state of being-in-love, but which you are now surprised to find have extremely little to do with what makes you go on loving him.

Nor is it altogether a maternal feeling that you have come to feel for him. In those perilously sweet pythonish kisses of yours there is a vein no doubt of diffused maternal sadism. But what you feel for him day in, day out, the feeling for him that runs parallel to your own private world, parallel to the "pleasure which there is in life and death," is something more than any maternal love. It is something for which there is no name save that tragically simple name "the love of women" which the Psalmist declares was "surpassed"—but peradventure he knew not what he said!—by the love of his friend.

Down at the bottom of all the "happiness" of both of them, when these two completely different creatures live together there lies this ultimate mystery, this mystery that is guarded by the woman's sacred duplicity, the fact that she loves him with a love for which there is no name, though all passion is dead, loves him, in spite of himself, for himself, but for a self of which he does not, in his masculine pride, even suspect the existence.

MAN WITH WOMAN

Man's private life—His fundamental fear—Woman's superiority in this respect—How man may defend his illusions—Retaining his stoical pride of thought—Woman the everlasting Hetaira—The anger of woman—The "in-spite-of" act—Exploiting the woman's emotions of fear and love—Other women—Keeping sensuality alive—Man's hidden dependence on woman.

IT APPEARS THAT IT IS EASIER FOR A MAN TO LIVE with a woman of whom he is fond, after the glamour of first love has faded, than it is for a woman to live with a man; and this seems to be because men are more detached from Nature than women, less involved in the little things of daily life, and much more pre-occupied with matters that have nothing to do with emotional association. It must be remembered that this work is more concerned with the problem of how to be happy than with the problem as to whether we have a right, in a world like this, to be happy at all.

I have tried to touch upon this other problem— our right to be happy in an unhappy world—in my chapter about conscience, where I sought to prove that not only have we a right to be so, but a mystical obligation to be so; but just as in Machiavel's "Prince" the moral aspects of tyranny are deliberately subordinated to the practical problem of how to be a successful tyrant, so in this book, if it is once granted that we have a right, and even an obligation, to be happy in spite of the miseries of other entities, the discussion, based on this assumed right, cannot be repeatedly tinkering at its moral foundation. It must go ahead shamelessly with the edifice it is erecting, treating personal happiness as the supremely desirable thing, and concerned solely with the technique of attaining it and with its quality when attained.

This matter of the right of an individual soul at least to *struggle* to be happy, when cases of unhappiness are constantly in its presence, is particularly applicable to the problem now before us by reason of the mysterious ways—at least from the viewpoint of the masculine consciousness—in which women, for causes obscure to the intelligence of man, seem often to cherish and foster their unhappiness as if it were suckling babe.

But even in cases where a man's affection for his partner is deep and tender the soul within him is just as solitary a Being as the soul within her and has, apart from anything her soul may be feeling, its own private and secret relation with the universe and with the mystery behind the universe. The solemn words of Jesus to his parents remain as an eternal protest on behalf of the ultimate independence of the individual soul and they are words that bear a peculiar significance when you consider what an intense temptation it is to a woman to invade, like the in-rushing of an ocean-wave, every cranny of her man's nature, until the very centre of his inmost being seems in danger of being surrounded by the swallowing tide.

I wonder how far women realise the part played in a man's consciousness by the Fear of Life. There are of course justifications for the traditional view that women are more nervous and more fearful than men; and experience bears witness to the little obvious particular fears in a feminine existence, but what might be called the *fear-skin* of humanity is really much thinner with men than with these soft bodies and troubled nerves at their side! The dullest man for instance has in him a thousand imaginative fears quite unknown to women. I would go so far as to say that with their realism and their never-ceasing sense of the underlying tragedy of things they are a great deal braver than men.

Men down at the bottom of their hearts *are afraid of life itself*. I suspect that they often have an obscure feeling, quite unknown to women, of belonging to a world of ideas and theories and purposes altogether outside the dark chaotic swirl of Nature's life-stream. With their human "fear-skin" so much thinner than women's men are forced to surround themselves with all manner of mental swaddling-bands. Like Caesar Augustus, who we learn from Suetonius had to swathe his body, beneath his grand armour, with rolls of flannel, every man instinctively uses his theories, his purposes, his hobbies, his ideals, down to his inmost life-illusion, as wrappings against this reality-terror which never quite leaves him.

It is this that gives a woman such power over her man; for she quickly becomes aware not only of the cracks in his world-armour, but of the ragged places in his interior swaddling-bands; and when she wants to hurt him, as she does in her moments of nervous anger, she can turn on these weak spots not only her own devastating insight but a thin black jet out of the recesses of the cosmos. Moving like a phosphorescent fish in the sub-aqueous tides of Nature she possesses a fatal power of squirting between the seams of his diver's dress this terrible fear-fluid sucked up from the ocean-floor.

As Shakespeare shows in Macbeth men are less prone to nervous troubles than women, but much more prone to imaginative troubles.

More women commit suicide from emotional

despair than men; but it is almost always some black jet of imaginative terror squirted between the joints of their rational harness that drives men to kill themselves.

Our atrocious English custom of flogging prisoners in extreme cases has, at the moment I am writing, caused one convict to hang himself with his shirt and another to swallow a fork, whereas women condemned to a similar torture would have been spared these imaginative spasms partly because their fear-skin is less thin and they never pad themselves with so much protective reasoning, and partly because they abide with, and seldom altogether forget, the basic atrocities of life itself.

Why is it that blunter, cruder, more obtuse men seem able to be happier in living with a woman than their more subtle brothers? Is it not because a certain vein of rough, crude brutality in their nature gives a woman the feeling—sometimes quite an erroneous feeling—that it were useless to turn upon an animal as rough-and-ready as this her deadly jet of ocean-floor secretion?

The more imaginative a man is—and all men are more imaginative than women—the more complicated will he find his life with any one of them. In one sense his imagination gives him—as far as his personal happiness is concerned—a tremendous advantage. I refer to his power to live a double life.

Now by "living a double life" I do not mean keeping hidden-up another woman. I mean keeping hidden-up *another mental life*. The more imaginative he is the more vivid this other mental life will be and the more complete escape it will be.

What hypocritical lies are passed round among us about the power of love! It may be wrong to be happy in a world like this except with the kind of side-ways happiness that comes to a saint, or at any rate to someone forever occupied in alleviating pain, but if we *have* decided to aim at happiness, it is moral cowardice not to face the situation in its starkest form.

To an extremely imaginative man—for we will drop the word "sensitive" since in matters of money and vanity and hunger and desire we are all "sensitive" and indeed we invariably notice that it is the most selfish people who talk most of their "sensitiveness"—the anger of women is more terrifying than women realise. It is like an explosion from that awful sub-world of Reality against which men are always padding themselves like the White Knight in "Alice through the Looking Glass," or like Caesar Augustus going to war.

And of course the more dreadful to an imaginative man is that sight of the Valkyrie storm-flash in a woman's face, that Pantherish darkening of the pupils, that Babylonian narrowing of the eyelids, the more often will he be exposed to it. And this will be brought about not because she is essentially cruel, but because the mere sight of his fear has an irritating effect upon her nerves.

Women are so close to Nature that they are far more belligerent than men. This is simply because they are more emotional; and, life being what it is, their emotions are naturally those of battle. Every woman is forever egging on her too-easily pacified mate to fight more fiercely for his own hand. And this eternal belligerency in the woman is by no means confined to clashes with other women, or even to clashes with other human beings. If you watch the animation of a woman's face when she is talking you will find that it radiates its intensest joy of life when she is loving something or hating something.

A man talks to show off, to cover his retreat, to save his face, to insert another cushion of rational argument between himself and the pricks of life. But talk from a woman is not an escape or a protection, or a palliative. It is an organic necessity. It is using her fins and her tail in life's ocean-stream. What she really does is to add her own terrifying reality to the reality of Nature. Actresses though they are, you will be astonished to note when you listen to a woman telling a story how passionately scrupulous she is about adherence to every smallest detail.

Here indeed is a significant revelation as to what interests them in life. Just simply Reality! They are reality-addicts, reality-inebriates. And you can prove this by encouraging any woman to let herself go in telling a tale. What thrills them so is that things should be as they are, people as they are, Life as it is. That sublime point to which Nietzsche rose with an effort that broke his brain, the point of not only enduring fate but "loving" fate—*amor fati*—is the natural and normal temperature of a woman's being. They *love* fate! They hate it too. They love it and hate it at the same time.

That a person's fate is his own character is what at the bottom of his heart the veriest ninny of a man takes for granted. That is why most successful men are so pompous and touchy. They think they've done it themselves. But no woman thinks she's done it herself. How can she, when she has responded with so much love and so much hate to the process of chance or destiny doing it?

Deeper down by far than anything else, in this question as to how a man is to be happy with a woman, when the state of being-in-love is over, is the matter of a man's life—fear which so naturally turns into his woman-fear.

When he listens to the outpouring of her love-hate

upon every detail in life, when he contemplates the intensity of her *amor-odium fati* over what to him seem the merest bagatelles, when he recognises in himself the heavy-witted, bewildered absent-mindedness, from which, like the denizen of a world of fantasy descending from a buoyant air-ship into wet salt waves, he makes his idiotic comments upon her reality, he feels as if she were confusing *him* with the wrong-doing fate she is denouncing so fiercely! It is at such times that he wonders to himself whether they would not both of them be happier if he could be her woman-friend by day, and her lover only at night.

The truth is that every woman has in her the makings of a realistic novelist, but a novelist with the imaginative art of selection left out. But why, indeed, should she select, when everything, simply *because it is there,* is a matter of absorbing and infinite interest to her?

It is the same in all classes of life. You have to go to a woman if you want to get the actual pressure of some event that has transpired or is transpiring, in the full pell-mell of all its chaotic details, whereas it is to a man you go if you want that selective imaginative touch, which, by a process of selection, gives the event its aesthetic impressiveness.

It is for this reason that when a man is telling you anything his woman will be forever interrupting him; for it is an actual pain to her to hear him leave out so many of the details in his artistic desire to make a hit.

But to come to the main issue of this chapter, how best can a man, the maker and defender of illusions, be happy in sharing bed and board day in, day out, with such an excoriating passionist of Reality? First let me hasten to say this. There are ways by which the imaginative power of men, even of the most simple men, can undermine a woman's passion for the flow of separate things with the more naked and more austere "truth" of what you might call the abstract human situation. What I mean is this. When your woman is in a mood for pricking the bubble of your illusions with the bodkin of her reality, instead of defending your opinions, instead of making yourself responsible for the drifting frag-ments of your rational ark, instead of trying in your portentous way to save your floating cargo from the flood, say to yourself, "Here are we, two doomed flesh-covered skeletons, wasting precious moments in useless argument, while at any second one or both of us may be seized with some intolerable pain, crushed in some appalling accident, laid bare in some unspeakable exposure, hurled to an annihilation so absolute that it will be the same, as far as we are concerned, as if we had never lived!"

By considerations of this drastic and ultimate kind, by the turning, that is to say, of your imaginative reason upon the abstract human situation, you will undermine the devastating procession of chaotic details with which she is overpowering your well-rounded theories, and you will do it by a bedrock pessimism so stark and austere that all these "details" of hers become irrelevant.

I don't for a moment mean that you should reveal to her this grim glance of yours at the bed-rock human situation, thus abstracted from the distracting play of circumstance, for its appropriateness to the occasion would be totally missed, and in her way of reducing everything to a personal reaction she would simply accuse you of being in a gloomy mood. But the value of this mental dive of yours down to the bed-rock of the world, below the swish of her mermaid's tail, below the glittering phosphorus of her darting motions, will lie in the restoration of your philosophic amour-propre. Women are themselves completely devoid of this inner necessity to feel profound, but they know by instinct how important it is to a man; and the way for a man to retain it under her attacks is to let her think she has pricked his conceit of it, while all the while he is lying *perdu* in a pessimistic vision of things so stark and ultimate that nothing can reach him. To grow increasingly happier in life a man *must* hug the pride of his mental stoicism; but the closer he can get this abstract virtue into some relation with reality the better for him.

To be happy in this hard world he *must* think of himself as a stoical philosopher whose virtue looks for no recognition beyond the inner glow which he gets from it; but he had better keep a weather-eye open, while he indulges in this secret pride, for various revelations about life that reach him through his woman.

Bewildered though he may be by her terrible insight into that life-flood of devastating details, he must keep his head enough to be able to gratify her by looking more of the unmasked fool, to which in her nervous irritation with his complacency she wishes to reduce him, than he actually feels, though he does not feel *quite* comfortable. But under her troublesome details, that seem to him to contradict all philosophy, the best thing he can do is to sink down through "reality" into what might be called "truth."

Reality is what appears. Truth is what our reason assures us lies behind appearances. I have recommended a pessimistic view of "truth" as more conducive to a man's pride of thought than an optimistic "truth," but as long as he keeps his thoughts to himself this latter will also serve.

Behind the philosophy of every masculine thinker,

and this applies as much to the ones who write books as to the ones who only patronize their women in conversation, lies, as my brother Theodore always says, the glory of pride.

Those who regard such pride of thought—even the pride of an extremely pessimistic view of things —as a masculine weakness and set themselves to destroy it in themselves, are taking a great risk. They usually end in a very unhappy state of mind. Now it is true that such an unhappy state of mind *may,* in a spiritual sense, be nobler than the proudest and most austere stoicism, but, as I have repeatedly hinted, what I am concerned with here is happiness, not nobility: happiness, I admit, of a certain *quality,* but still happiness in preference to unhappiness.

Thus if it turns out, as I think it does, that in a world of petty miseries like ours a masculine nature —devoid of the feminine passion for appearances —must, to struggle on at all, derive an inward glow from feeling its stoical self-control grow more and more effective, it will be madness in him to try to destroy this ancient classic pride.

But perhaps he *is* mad compared with other men! Perhaps he feels driven on by some spiritual urge to attack this simple stoical pride of his at its very root.

Well! let me for the last time gravely warn him of the terrible danger to his happiness along this path. He is acting contrary, or I should say feeling contrary, to the essential nature of a man. But on the other hand, if he is subtle enough, the thing is possible. A man *can* relinquish his natural pride, and the subtlest of the Chinese sages—namely, the great Taoists—supply us with a crafty technique for this very thing, without suffering unhappiness, but the process is such an evasive one, and such an elusively spiritual one, that only very rare souls can follow it without losing everything.

But the Tao does not offer the *only* path to this difficult secret. There is also the Christian "way," by which I mean the way, not of Bunyan's Pilgrims, for *their* virtue is made up of fear and pride, but of certain among the older Catholic saints.

But since my immediate problem is how a man can be happy while he eats and sleeps with so strangely-constituted a creature as a woman, and since when a saint becomes a saint he gives up living with women, it becomes necessary to use a technique that has no formal religious precedent.

Women it is true have a penchant for saints, but they also have an irresistible urge to disturb their sanctity; and the best and most modern thing to aim at, it seems to me, if you are really resolved to give up your inmost pride, is something more on the lines of Dostoievsky's Idiot or, if you prefer, of Alyosha Karamazov. The Idiot certainly succeeded

in killing his inmost pride. What at the bottom of
his nature, then, really was his life-illusion? This is
a hard question, but it is spiritually of the greatest
importance to us just here, when we are making a
desperate struggle to acquire a life-illusion of our
own that goes against the whole grain of our masculine nature.

The attempt we are making now is indeed one of
the most perilous that a masculine soul could possibly make, as far as his happiness is concerned, and
yet I do not think it would be correct to call the
Idiot an unhappy person.

It were certainly easier for a man, in these sceptical times, to follow the spiritual path of the Idiot,
than to make the wild and desperate clutch after
Christian humility described with such tragic and
beautiful passion by St. Paul in the words "Not I—
but Christ in me."

What you get in the Idiot is such an abysmal sense
of "the equality of all souls" in the presence of the
terrible and beautiful mystery of life, that this feeling of being "a Superior Man" as the Chinese say,
or of being at any rate a much-enduring stoical man,
which is what most men are conscious of, is struck
by lightning at its root. What penetrated the soul
of the Idiot was a constant vivid awareness of the
tragic beauty of every human soul he encountered;
and when, as on the occasion of that fashionable

party when he broke the vase, any human group behaved in the remotest way decently he was stirred to the profoundest depths of his soul. What the Idiot seems to have felt was *a sensation of identity* between his souls and the souls of others, so that he both rejoiced with them and suffered with them, and when his two women, Nastasya and Aglaia, quarrelled so violently over him, he had no choice but to take the side of the one he loved with pity against the one he loved with love because the nerve of your pity goes further in self-identification with the object than does the more normal feeling of amorous attraction.

Spengler speaks mysteriously of some new religious sense, just born into the world, which he associates with the Fourth Gospel and with the character of Alyosha Karamazov; but most seekers after new spiritual methods of making life more tolerable, particularly life *à deux,* will I think agree with me that it is easier to grasp what the Idiot is feeling in the depths of his heart and the method he is following than it is to get any definite philosophic notion of Alyosha's system of life. I feel about Alyosha as if he were one of those super-sturdy, super-practical, naturally affectionate angels that you see in so many early Italian pictures, nor can I feel that Alyosha has as deep an understanding of the evil that surrounds him as the Idiot has.

We are wandering in deep waters here in our masculine search for some thaumaturgic clue—like Faust's key to the subterranean dwelling of "the Mothers"—that will initiate us into a life-illusion that can dispense with moral and mental pride, and the great danger is that the moment a man relinquishes his sturdy, heathen, self-righteous, self-centered stoicism, and allows the feelings of alien souls to disturb him to the depths, in the way the Idiot did, he will find that at a crisis he is neither a self-contained stoic, nor a tragically sympathetic medium for the Love of Christ; but simply a poor wandering "nebula" of bewildered human consciousness, *sans* centre, *sans* circumference, *sans* background, *sans* all steady and integral continuity.

I fully admit that even in this fluid and formless state his soul may—though unknown to itself—gain some deep and mystic "rapport" with the rank and file of humanity. Indeed the feeling of being lost amid the tossed and troubled waves in the great sea of tragic human life, *may* bring with it some strange unlooked for ecstasy of *identification with All Souls* and with their pitiful destiny, just as Alyosha fell down with rapturous sobs and kissed the earth, in spite of the fact that his friend's corpse had begun to stink; but in spite of such isolated moments of chance-sent rapture there is a serious danger that you will soon just begin to drift at random

— 163 —

through life, trusting to your inspired moments to thrill you and keep you going, and then suddenly find yourself, a besotted slave of some mania, some madness, some vice, some drug, some obsession, followed by misery and unhappiness, to which if you had retained your moral pride, and had been still practising your self-righteous stoicism, you would never have submitted.

But since we are considering the problem as to how a man can live most happily with a woman why should we not ask the question, "Why can't he imitate women's attitude to life?" Women very rarely indulge themselves in pride of thought or in pride of stoical self-control. They often pity themselves as the victims of chance or fate or of some malignant and selfish man; but they seldom think of themselves with complacency as philosophic stoics.

And this freedom from the pride of virtue saves them from the misery of remorse. They don't feel remorse, because they are not concerned with the building up of an interior mental philosophy, the disturbance of which causes pain.

But if the Idiot's freedom from moral pride and Alyosha's freedom from moral pride are deep spiritual secrets, why should not women's freedom from this particular kind of egoism be an equally subtle clue? I think it *is* such a clue; only it is extraordinarily difficult for a man to make use of more than a very little of it, and even that only intermittently.

If you watch women closely you will notice how they fling themselves "entire" and "all-of-a-piece" into the particular emotion they are expressing. They have their reserves of course; and they are, by inescapable necessity, actresses and deceivers; but what they reserve is only *more of the same emotion* that they express, or some hidden store of a directly opposite emotion. Their reserve is in fact a reserve of themselves—of *more* of themselves—not, as with men, the reserve of an ego that is lying back on the pride of its moral values and on the superiority of its mental vision.

But what would be the effect upon a woman if a man really did set himself to destroy his secret masculine pride of thought? It is hard to say—certainly such a course, whether he followed the way of the saints, or the way of the Tao, or the way of Dostoievsky's idiot would take from her her greatest weapon for making him unhappy; but on the other hand if he removed her power of making him unhappy, he would also be denying her the greatest relief and release she has for her tense and vibrant nervous irritation.

This irritation really comes from the fact that deep in her heart she wants from you *the companion-*

ship of a woman combined with the stimulus and security of your being a man.

On the whole, for you *are* a man, it is safest, since you are more anxious to be happy than to make subtle spiritual experiments, to get as much comfort as you can out of your stoical pride of thought. After all it is this pride of thought that lies behind most of the progress, such as it is, that our race has won in its struggle with Nature. Women, being so intimate a part of nature, are indeed a microcosm of the great mysterious ocean over which a man is steering his raft; and it may well be that the Christian and Taoistic tricks of throwing overboard his pride of reason and his pride of stoical morality is a kind of cosmic betrayal of man's proper destiny.

It is certainly a giving up of that essential detachment, that isolation in the fortress of his lonely thinking-power, which has made him all the way down history the grand Observer of Nature, and the grand Meddler with Nature. Grant then, that if you want to be happy with a woman it is safer to remain the egoistic philosopher and moralist you were born, and that Heraclitus and Socrates and Epictetus and Epicurus and Goethe and Nietzsche were born, rather than to play any subtle oriental tricks with some dark inhuman secret of humility. But all the same it does still remain that the deeper you force your pride of thought and your pride of virtue to sink down out of sight into your soul the less you will suffer unhappiness and the less you will quarrel with your woman.

But the man is unwise who—because he is struck by the tidal recurrences and reversions of his woman's loves and hates, and because he finds in her no sort of moral standards resembling his own —comes to the conclusion that women have nothing in them that corresponds to his morality. He has forgotten that beautiful Athenian word for an intellectual paramour which is the feminine counterpart of the Homeric word comrade. Women's natures are not, as various masculine philosophers have erroneously argued, composed entirely of maternal psychology and courtesan psychology. There is still in all of them an indestructible element of brooding romance, or rather of that unconscious passivity, hushed, inscrutable, virginal, inarticulate, that their first lover, moving like the creative spirit "on the face of the waters," troubled with the reciprocity of love.

It is this same mystic element in their nature, only with a new quality added, that returns upon them, deep as life itself, when they are nursing their first child.

But though men catch the virginal romance of this feminine mystery in the face of the young girl they love, and again in the face of the mother of their child, there is something in this thing that is different from mere innocence and different from mere maternity. It partakes of the mystery of that strange brooding expectancy that we are aware of sometimes in Nature, when we seem to catch certain aspects of her life unawares and offguard.

Now there exists something of this hushed submental passivity, where you feel that her thoughts are as vague and obscure, and as deep too, as physical feelings, in every woman, and it is from this unfading element in her, the very thing that so roused his romantic interest at the first, that a man, who wishes to get the full intense flavour of his privilege of spending days and nights with this strange Being, must draw the living water of his life. For there is a mystery here more evasive than all her courtesan provocations and all her maternal obsessions. And it is the thing in her that neither her momentary angers can touch, nor her possessiveness dispel. It is something which the passing of the years has no power to diminish.

But it is a sacred thing, perhaps the most sacred of all; and it has always to be approached, by the man who recognises it, over a bridge as narrow and enchanted as that which led to the Castle of the Grail.

But this mystic passivity, which is the cause of all sexual romance, and which, for a man with any

will-power in his imagination, can never lose its
appeal, is not the only quality in women that belongs neither to the courtesan nor the mother. There
is also a woman's psychic sympathy. This is that
large, calm, soothing, restorative power, like the
cool stone rim of a fairy fountain, for the sake of
which men in all times have come to a certain type
of woman. And they have always found what they
sought, were she a cup-bearer serving drinks or a
wrinkled crone stirring a pot on the fire or a baya-
dere at rest after her dance, or an Aspasia pondering on the secrets of human life. They have found
the woman who can be a companion. A man is
aware of this mystery, this sympathy as deep as
Nature herself, in the most unlikely quarters. He
can feel it in the face of a barmaid at the counter,
in the face of a beggar on the street, in the look of
a patient shop-girl, in the presence of a great lady
weary with the handling of huge assemblies of
guests, in the hushed quiescence of an over-worked
charwoman.

It is not the response of the courtesan, nor is it
the response of the mother. It is something deeper,
more organically feminine than either of these. An
old maid can display it, who is totally devoid of
amorous provocation and entirely free from maternal emotion. It is the sympathy of the Eternal
Companion, of the undying Helper, of the everlast-

ing *Hetaira*. It is the thing that makes a man call a casually-encountered woman "sister." In a certain sense it *is* the sister-quality, but the sister-quality with something added. Almost all nuns possess it, and so do almost all prostitutes.

And when a man comes, for understanding and for clairvoyant insight into his special needs, to a woman in this mood it would be absurd to say she is devoid of "morality." She is devoid of his pompous logical morality but she has something deeper, more flexible, more instinctive and far more precious. She has her own special system—though it is not at all what a man means by a "system"—of deep social values. It would be giving this quality a too pedantic air to call it the quality of a teacher; and yet there does adhere to it a deep touch of the teacher—shall I say of the Sibyl?—and happy are the men who have the wisdom to put themselves to school in this informal Sibylic "academia!"

Now a man who lives with the woman he has been in love with will, if he cares for his happiness at all, exploit this element in his companion to the uttermost. And he will find that a woman, playing the part of a real companion is no more devoid of something corresponding to his "reason" than she is devoid of something corresponding to his "morality." She may turn away to her sewing, or to her market-basket, or to her curtains or her china, or

even to her game of Patience, when she listens to
the duller, the more logical aspects of her man's
reiterated thoughts; but when by any chance his
ideas touch the intense and quivering magnet-needle
of a real encounter of electric currents her whole
nature vibrates in response.

Who are the human souls who answer with alert
intelligence to every great new mystic and aesthetic
idea? The souls of women. Not only Jesus and
Mahomet and Confucius and Buddha, but Henry
James and Joyce and Proust and Dorothy Richardson will be found to have their first disciples among
women. The more purely logical systems of thought
from Spinoza to Einstein may suit men better than
women, but I doubt if any men-disciples were
quicker to catch the significance of such explorers
of new territory as Goethe and Wordsworth and
Blake and Carlyle and Nietzsche, than these great
men's mothers and sisters and wives and sweet-
hearts.

Women may be less on the alert about new schools
of sculpture and architecture and painting, but it
seems to me that they make up by far the larger
part of the audiences for new literature and new
music.

And who are the people ready to listen most in-
tently to any really exciting and critical illumina-
tions that average men have? Always women! And

this is because each particular man with any originality is far too self-centered to have leisure for the
thoughts of other men.

Any man really concerned with his deeper mental
happiness must constantly make a clean sweep of
all the little pinpricks of his life with his mate and
concentrate on those impersonal issues, to do with
life in general, where his reactions will be quite
different from hers, and where to analyse hers will
be for him like the reading of a thrilling book; for
compared with the life of a bachelor the life of a
man who lives with a woman is twice as rich, twice
as complicated, twice as interesting. "More interest,
more suffering," you will say, and this is true; but
the suffering in question, if the torture of jealousy
does not enter, is nothing compared with the imaginative terrors and morbid manias that a man escapes
when between him and the fearfulness of the cosmos there revolves this *other* disturbing and distracting stellar system. All life is a battle, full of
victories and defeats. How much better to have your
victories and defeats *under your hand,* than at this
ghastly long range, where you confront without a
shield the horrors of the infinite. Nothing makes for
the happiness of a man with a woman more effec-
tively than for him to understand the abysmal difference between his bursts of anger and hers, and
why it is essential for him to keep his temper, *but
not for her.*

A man's anger springs from his sense of justice. It arises when he feels that he is suffering from injustice, from some outrage to his code, to his bargain, to what is right and fair and according to the bond between them. It is an accumulative anger, "looking before and after," and covering in its scope a long reach of time.

A woman's anger, on the contrary, has to do with nerves, not reason, and, if you rule out jealousy, and jealousy will not arise if he confesses every lapse as it occurs save where his deception of her has been so complete that there is no chance of discovery, it springs primarily from her woman's irritation at his masculine limitations.

And, strange as this may seem, it is intimately connected with her love for him. In fact we could hazard the paradox that her bursts of anger *are part of the actual expression of her love*.

A man is simply a fool, and devoid of all insight, who takes seriously the wild and whirling words of his woman's anger, and solemnly places them at the bar of his sense of justice. She will say anything at such moments, anything that will hurt him; and she knows well—who better?—what will hurt him most. "You don't think I *meant* that?" she will say later, and it is true that she did not mean it in *his* sense; and he ought to have had the wit to understand this. But few men have; and so he makes himself unhappy, pondering on the injustice of her *thought,* when he ought to congratulate himself on this curious proof of the security and confidence of her love.

I have already indicated three mental acts which are of great use to a human soul when the misery of the "outward" assails it. The plunge into the darkness of the mystery behind life was the first of these and I named it the Ichthian act.

The second, which I named the act of De-carnation, was the trick by which you imagine your soul as something separate from your body, holding your body as if by a leash; while the third of these mental processes, which I called the Panergic act, was a vigorous grasping by the mind of all those primitive elemental pleasures which make life most tolerable to you.

But when your woman, as is bound to happen sometimes, when her nerves are on edge, sets herself to make you unhappy, or to pulverise your happiness with her unhappiness, I have yet another psychic device up my sleeve which may serve your turn better than any of the foregoing. This I call the "In-spite-of" act; and if you get into the habit of forcing yourself to make it when things are at the worst you will get great help and comfort.

The "In-spite-of" act is a desperate up-springing of your inmost soul, as if from the very pit of your stomach, by which you challenge the evils that surround you, including in this case your partner's bitter tongue, and defy them, in the strength of a Being possessing an auto-creative power.

This interior Being, in spite of what it is suffering, can still cry, "I am happy," while its world of familiar sensations cracks and sways and topples. It is a spiritual battle-cry, this "In-spite-of" act, rising up from your solitary navel. You utter it as if—and this is eminently satisfactory to your deepest self-respect —you were actually the ideal stoic philosopher who can abide "impavidum" while the *orbis terrarum* crashes about him. The "In-spite-of" act asks nothing, desires nothing, hopes nothing. It just asserts your own solitary will-power, bent on resistance and resolved to be cheerful at all cost. The best of this proud act of the soul is that it dispenses altogether with everything "outward." It does not remind you of your little pleasures, it does not separate your soul from your body; it utters its "de-profundis" cry, its solitary "Let there be Happiness!" as if it were itself the centre and circumference of everything that is.

But since, even while you are engaged on this desperate act of the soul, you behold your annoyed and annoying partner before you, and are forced to listen to her scathing words, it is best to yield completely to her in outward semblance. Yield, I say,

and again yield! Give her the satisfaction—why not?
—of thinking that she has hurt you to the heart, that
you are wounded and defenceless, that you are
humiliated, stripped, exposed.

The pleasure you derive from deceiving her in
this—for your humiliation from your own secret
point of view covers a thaumaturgic triumph—will
give you such an interior glow that you will feel an
intense wave of tenderness towards her. She also
will feel the glow of victory, will feel that she has
punished her boy-philosopher sufficiently and this
feeling will evoke in her a corresponding rush of
tenderness for you.

Thus the trouble between you will melt away and
a lovely harmony will ensue, a harmony that, like
so many other forms of human happiness, will be
rooted and grounded in deception.

Stern advocates of what is called "truth at all
costs" will utter a violent protest at the line I am
taking; but it must be remembered that in a world
like ours—a world so largely created by the various human thought-bubbles that we name "life-
illusions"—it often happens that a deception leaves
us really closer to the essential truth of things than
this ferocious and misleading honesty.

The truth at all costs is desirable enough in Science where human nature is not involved, but in
human relations, especially in the relations between

— 176 —

men and women, it is better, and even in a profound sense more "honest," to accept certain deceptions as inevitable.

For a man to be happy with a woman, he must get clearly into his head at the start that she cares nothing for his particular kind of morality and nothing for his particular kind of reason. When she is good it is because *her* emotions and *her* values are involved, and when she is bad it is because yours are involved.

But, you will say, why is it that there are so many quiet, patient, docile, submissive and long-suffering wives? I am afraid that the answer to this lies in the single word "fear."

Now the fear of women for men is a very different thing from the fear of men for women because it has a subtle pleasure in it. The physical hurt in the original sexual act from which such complicated mental ripples of masochism and sadism radiate to infinity, plays its part in this subtle pleasure, and there is also the satisfaction that *any* submission when touched with a vein of irony is able to produce. But however much pleasure may be mingled with a woman's fear of her man, the point is that good, docile wives are still actuated by secret emotions and values totally different from a man's reasonable concept of right and wrong.

And it is her susceptibility to emotion that a man

who wants to be happy with her must constantly exploit. It is the only way to get round her, the only way to make her behave decently. It is useless for him to try to understand *her* inner system of values. A man must either excite in her the emotion of fear —an emotion often pleasurable to her—or he must appeal to her emotion of love.

To try to excite her pity is a mistake; and here I touch upon a blunder that men are constantly making. They themselves are led to be very tender to their woman when they pity her, for pity is the most reasonable of all human feelings, is, in fact the inverse side of justice; but there is something annoying to a woman's nerves to be forced to pity the man she lives with, and this annoyance increases rather than diminishes her bad humour.

No, if you want to be happy with her the only way is to excite her emotion of fear—which is a much pleasanter thing *than your fear of her*—or to excite her emotion of love.

Never try to move her to pity, that inverse of justice, and never appeal to your own idea of the difference between right and wrong. Arnold Bennett says no man ever made himself and his woman happy by trying to base their life on justice, and I say it is almost as great a mistake to base it on pity.

Appeal to love or appeal to fear; for these are the motive-forces she understands. Like the black ashes of a burnt ledger-book she will fling to the winds all other considerations; and you will find that you have only made matters worse by introducing such irrelevancies.

And when I say "appeal to her love" I don't mean make cold-blooded rational speeches about it, for *that* will annoy her worst of all, as an appeal translated into *your* language and therefore becoming totally false.

You must, even in the midst of your sulkiness and her anger, "make the motion" of love, *whether you feel it or not,* and in "broken speech and your whole function suiting in form to this conceit" implore her to forgive you and be friends again.

The reason why women who have quarrelled with their men and left them feel themselves tempted to a vindictiveness more cruel than the grave is because in that place within their flesh and blood where they "possessed" you, and loved and hated their "possession," there is now a ghastly and hurting emptiness. They can no longer feel pulsing within them what they love and what they fear. They can only feel undying vindictiveness towards that emptiness in themselves which is now *all that you are.*

All men feel that it is absurd of women to have such contempt for men's pride of morality and pride of philosophical stoicism, for they feel that women have no idea to what brutal and callous lengths men *could* go if this pride of virtue in them did not hold them back!

And what mood is it that these stoical men do sometimes allow themselves as a substitute for the physical violence that their morality forbids. Well! *they sulk.* Now it is clear that no philosopher dealing with the problem of happiness can deny that women get a definite pleasure out of the expression of anger—"Anger," says the masculine proverb "is short madness"; but to women it is a balm, a nepenthe, a release, a relief, a divine comfort to their nerves and a consummation of all their suppressed feelings.

It is a sign of a happy life! A really unhappy woman is beyond the panacea of getting angry. But a man's sulking is a very different thing. He derives no pleasure from it; it is a release of nothing; it is a balm for nothing. To sulk is one of the meanest of all masculine ways. It plagues your woman much more than an outburst of anger; but you must not suppose it puzzles her or is calculated to bring her round; for it is on a precise par with the behaviour of that simple boy-child to whose mental proportions she loves reducing you.

But there is, I believe, no effort of the will that man, the great Moralist, can possibly make, equal to the effort of breaking the ice of his own sulkiness before it has become solid enough to bear his weight. It is in matters like this that a philosopher really can do something to increase the happiness of his woman and himself. Never argue with her, unless in the spirit of a chess champion playing with a beautiful savage. And never sulk, when—as you ought to have foreseen would inevitably happen— she gets the better of you and humiliates you.

The great thing on both sides, if a man and a woman are to be happy together, is for them each to be themselves to the limit. So many of our modern intellectual ménages, if an association can be called a ménage that is as hugger-mugger as a circus-camp, are rendered unhappy because the man thinks that it is unintellectual to be masculine, and the woman thinks it is unintellectual to be feminine. They struggle to be the distorted victims of intellectual modernity and intellectual sincerity, when all that is needed to make them happy is a taste of Helen of Troy's Egyptian Nepenthe; in other words a drop of that primeval Duplicity which Nature herself pours like a blessed oil upon her sexes.

Let the woman therefore give way freely to all those furious tempers that she calls her "nerves" and that are the tax humanity has to pay for the complicated organism that brings it into being. And let the man indulge himself without scruple or hesitation in his pride of being crafty and much enduring.

Let every woman, in other words, be the natural

Penelope *she* is, and every man the natural Odysseus *he* is.

I hinted in my last chapter that a woman's happiness in life depends first on her creative atmosphere-making, and secondly on her success in the delicate art of swallowing her mate whole; and I suggested at the same time that if a man is cunning enough to slip off into his own secret mental world when this swallowing process is going on he will not mind the feeling of being reduced to boyhood again in order to be small enough to vanish within that Lamia-skin.

I have often thought what a pity it is that the penetrating ideas of D. H. Lawrence about the relations between men and women should be confined to their state when they are still in the first condition of "being-in-love." My own problem in this book is quite different; for I have to indicate the technique by which Lady Chatterley and her "tour-de-force" lover can be happy together when those first bewildering adjustments are over. With regard to that early state of "being-in-love" I hold my peace, for a super-happiness enters into *that,* which is totally beyond philosophic analysis.

Even Socrates, in Plato's famous Symposium, needed the word of the Sibyl before he could describe that mystic union.

I have a notion however that certain portions of my technique will have their value for young people who are "keeping company" but have not yet risked the plunge; and I am the bolder in saying this because I feel that *something*, a little anyway of the ideal unity the boy is conscious of is not as completely shared by his more realistic companion as he imagines. She instinctively takes her colour and her cue from her ideas and she is not less preoccupied and bemused than he; but being a woman she "keeps her head," as Shakespeare makes Juliet do, and never quite loses her grasp upon the practical aspect of affairs.

If a man has not the airy conscience of a Don Juan—and the ironical thing is that almost all women deep in their hearts, owing I suppose to their innate lack of masculine morality, have a secret admiration for this irresponsible rogue—he may well regard it as a tragic thing that his natural lust for the sweetness of femininity should thus land him in a situation so fraught with perils to his happiness. To be attracted by the exquisite delight of making love to the incredible yieldingness of an enchanted body, only to discover—when he comes to live with this body—that he has landed himself with a personality ten times more belligerent than he is, is a startling shock to most young men.

What he loved was girlhood in the abstract, or

beauty in the abstract, but what is now bent on possessing him, body and soul, is a mysterious and strange Being, whose ways are not *his* ways, neither her thoughts *his* thoughts.

Let modern methods of liberation go as far as they may, there is one thing they cannot liberate a girl from, and that is her woman's nature; and just as this nature exists under the most fashionable and courtly attire, so does it exist under the most Bohemian disarray.

Had Bill Sikes not murdered his Nancy, had he been a little less of a callous brute, that young lady would not have confined her possession of him to the possession of a few of his trade secrets.

What then is the "possessed" male to do? *That* is the rub. The greatest obstacle to a man's happiness with a woman is the accumulated weight of all the little *contretemps* of everyday life, for, since a woman takes these things twice as hard as a man, he not only has to bear whatever weight of vexation they would cause him if he lived alone, but a good share of the far heavier weight they bring down upon her.

Well! The only thing for him to do is to repress all real deep anxious concern over her special feminine aggravations. If he yielded to this his own life-happiness would not be worth an owl's pellet. Nor in his wretchedness would his woman pity him be-

— 184 —

cause since she has the power of being worried to death one moment and full of radiant good spirits the next, she instinctively feels that rage against the little worries of life and a lively zest for the little pleasures of life are both of the essence of life; and certainly the cosmos would not pity him. In fact he would have crossed the No Man's Land from his own emotional trench to the woman's only to lose *his* protective weapons and not be able to use hers.

Next to the little daily annoyances, what is most disturbing to a man's happiness under these conditions is the problem of other people—particularly of other women. He is jumpy and suspicious about her attitude to these other women, whether relatives or otherwise, and she observing his suspiciousness grows, by natural contrariness, more recklessly herself than before. Watching her in his furtive ambassadorial way, he will be tempted to bring to bear upon her least nervous reaction, her least emotional spasm, the whole camel's load of men's grievances against women since the beginning of the world. He will mutter to himself, "They must have blood; they must and *will* have blood!" And he will watch her so closely that all her free spontaneous sallies, for and against these other women—sallies which it is her nature to utter "for and against" everything in the world—appear to him in the sinister light of a demand for blood.

But what is he to do? She *does* seem to him to be coaxing out of him every detail she can get about these other women, their looks, their ways, their habits, their weaknesses. She seems driven on by that mysterious psychic yearning that Dostoievsky disclosed in his Aglaia; *to get as near as possible* to these women; to get to the point of embracing them; to get to the point of flowing like a mist round their inmost identity.

Well! what is his attitude to be towards these feminine peculiarities? Is he to hunt them down, as Strindberg did, shooting his malicious arrows at them before their white tails can vanish into their burrows?

Or is it conclusive to his happiness to take the larger, more generous, more indulgent attitude, the attitude, in fact, that might be called Shakespearean? It seems to me that he will be rewarded for this magnanimous view of things—even at the risk, as Pascal might put it, of sprinkling himself with holy water, till he gets stupid by not only feeling tenderer towards her than is possible when he is watching her like an inspired bed-bug, but by remaining sensitive to that magical charm of her femininity which the particular insight I have alluded to tends to under-rate.

What he must recognise is that this Being at his side has burnt her ships in committing herself to him in a more tragic sense than he has any conception of. He must realise that she has given herself to him—below all their quarrels—to an extent that has a terrible finality, a finality far beyond the implication of anything she says or does. He must realise the miraculous power within her of bringing children out of Limbo into mortal existence is something that—whether she uses it or not—sinks their relation to each other *as far as she is concerned* into an under-tide of startling and dreadful mystery, wherein, as if through a crack in a great weir, the waters of death mingle with the waters of life. And thus it comes about that if she finds he is deceiving her with another woman something happens in the under-world of her secret life to which he can never get the real clue; no! not if he reason with her for a thousand years!

She may be as "modern" as you can please in the rational ideas of our scientific age. Something there is in the mystery of Nature that refuses to be modernised; and to that something she is closer than all the philosophers in the world.

It is not his desire for another woman that will ruin their happiness. It is not even his possession of another woman. It is her discovery that he has deceived *her*. For these reasons if he wishes to go on living with her and retain his happiness there is only one thing to do and that is to confess. It is natural and right that he should deceive her in a thousand ways; but he runs a terrible risk if he deceives her over another woman.

It is, after all, the Strindberg in him, not the Shakespeare, the malicious half-feminine man, not the indulgent imaginative man, who now says to himself, "She must have blood!"

But whether it be "blood" or lavender-water, if you want to be happy with your One-of-all you must offer up *something* to her that belongs to the other woman; not necessarily that other's whole wardrobe, but a ribbon or two, a shoe-lace, a safety-pin, a powder-box, a glove. You will feel remorse. You will feel a scoundrel. You will also feel a fool. But it is better to be a shameless fool in Paradise than a discreet and honourable gentleman in Hell.

I would not bid you to offer on the altar even this little pin-prick of the other woman's life unless it were absolutely essential for your happiness to do so. But after all what the other woman loses is only this thimble-full of pride, whereas if you go on letting your mate feel you are deceiving her you are doing something to her soul in a dimension of terrible mystery totally beyond your plumb-line's fathoming. It is curious to note the impersonal malice that men feel towards women and what intense malicious joy they take in dissecting their frailties; and if you analyse to the bottom your scrupulous protection of one woman from another woman I believe you will find that it often springs not from a sense of honour at all but from pure maliciousness. It isn't that you love this other woman so much; but that you derive a wicked joy from *not* giving your girl the witch's pleasure of sticking pins into the wax image of her rival!

There is a vague notion in most men's minds that it removes personal bitterness and makes things happier all round if they mentally vent their spleen on *Women in General* when their mate torments them. As a student of the greatest of all arts I regard this method as a grave mistake. By far the better way is to allow yourself in your mind to indulge in a savage orgy of thinking of your woman as the worst and wickedest of all women.

Give yourself up to thinking of everything about her that annoys you most. And then—when you have gone to the limit—swing round to the opposite extreme and think of her as you love her best, as you admire her most, all her faults forgotten. By indulging yourself in the first of these extreme views you will satisfy your suppressed indignation and you will feel a delicious reaction in her favour just as if you had struck her into insensibility. And then when you build up her image again out of all the elements you love best in her, it will be as if she had died and come to life.

The great thing is to assume in the depths of

your mind that it is impossible for her to change but always possible for *you* to change. Be an absolute fatalist about her, and a believer in absolute free will in regard to yourself. This is a secret attitude that will cause a warm proud glow to irradiate your stoic mind, and it will make you as indulgent to her as if she were some elemental force of Nature that must be accepted without question.

And as day follows day never let yourself cease to be vividly aware of all the little material adjustments she makes that are so necessary to your comfort.

I will not go so far as to say that the orderly smoothness and rhythmic harmony of all these little things are what give a man's mind the necessary leisure wherein to enjoy the pride of his detachment, for there are plenty of hermit-bachelors who do their own housework after their fashion, and do it, too, with a fresh and child-like zest that makes of these things a religious ritual, a ritual that enhances rather than lessens the detached pleasure of thought.

Though women get such a deep creative satisfaction from their "atmospheric" effects, they are too involved in the whole thing to be able to derive that particular childish pride in what they are doing that men enjoy. They do these things in such a "grown-up" manner and they take them so much for granted that a man is led to wonder in amazement at the sight of what to him seems mere ritual and mere play being made into such an organic necessity.

But if he is to be happy in the presence of all this, if he is to keep his self-respect in the presence of all this, the only thing for him to do is to sink deeper and deeper into his own secret world.

And she herself, her innate femininity contemplated from the detached stand-point of his free mind, becomes one of the chief elements in this secret world!

Their first rapturous epoch of love-making over, if the man is to be happy he must aim at increasing, quickening, and forever stimulating that magical lust, half-sensual and half-psychic, which a woman's body and the flickering expressions on a woman's face have the power of exciting in him.

It is a great mistake to suppress in his secret mind his attraction to the other woman he casually encounters. The thing to do is to use every passing glimpse he may snatch of these other longed-for caskets of mystery to enhance diffused satisfaction in the one at his side. She is his "bird in the hand," and he is a poor philosopher, and one with a miserably weak imagination, who cannot day after day, and night after night, enjoy this "bird in the hand" as a living embodiment of all the infinite allurements which so attract him.

For the grand secret of a man's continuous happiness with a woman is to keep his imaginative sensuality vividly alert and alive. For her sake he has isolated himself from his relatives and friends, for her sake he has compromised with his morality, with his philanthropy, with his pathetic fumblings after mystical sanctity.

But if he is a master of himself and his feelings he now has his reward. He has got this Microcosm of Nature at his disposal, at his mercy, at his pleasure, and for the infinite enjoyment of his imaginative senses.

This immodest book is, if you will, a Devil's Hand-Book of Happiness, and Machiavel's Breviary of the Passing Hours. Let a man, therefore, see to it that when he makes love to his mate he finds a substitute for the old rapture of Platonic fusion in a new rapture of satyrish divergence. To get the full happiness of dallying with her and enjoying her he were wise to merge the identity of the form he knows so well into an impersonal "Imago" of the Eternal Feminine. He has suffered from her lack of *his* kind of morality; let him now take full advantage of this. His innate idealism has always been a trouble to her, disturbing the practical sagacity of her life.

Well! Let him cast away this idealism where he makes love to her and exploit her abysmal indifference to these niceties. He may be sure of one thing. It is only in books that the best of women are shocked by satyrish sensuality. The best of women offer their bodies with sympathetic indifference as a sweet sacrifice to every kind of sensuality in their mate.

And no triumph of the life-spirit over the death-spirit is greater than for a couple who have once been lovers to remain satyr and oread right on to the verge of old age.

A man for whom his "old girl" when her youthful bloom is gone is still "Girlhood in the Abstract," is the master-adept in the Eleusinian Mysteries of love.

But I have left the uttermost secret of a man's happiness with his woman to the end of this chapter. Parallel with those feelings in her when she reduces his tall form to a size that she can hold between her hands and possess with her lips and her breasts and her whole physical being, is the unutterable tenderness that suffuses the man's nature when he sees her familiar form and face under certain particular aspects. Especially is this true of the moments when he catches her asleep. Indeed many times when he detects upon her face a certain wistful and virginal expression he feels towards her *as if she were asleep.* In other words he catches the frail pulse-beat of her essential and heart-breaking femininity as if it hovered between life and death, as if this incalculable and equivocal changeling of Nature were suspended between the poignance of what the loss of her would be and the poignance of her strange impossible livingness!

In this whole matter of a man's happiness *à deux* when the state of "being-in-love" is over, the strangest thing is the obscure and unconscious depth of his hidden dependence upon her. This dependence upon her resembles the dependence of all the men "who eat bread upon the earth" on the elements that feed them.

It is something that gives to a man's conscious happiness a deep unconscious foundation.

Against this background his happiness grows and flourishes but the tragedy is that his awareness of it so often does not come *till he loses her*. To be fully happy with her, then, he had better constantly imagine what life would be without her. For without being aware of it the tendrils and fibres, the stalks and filaments of his organic life have sunk so deep into that soft, tender, sympathetic, but at the same time disturbing and troubling soil, that they have rooted themselves there.

His real feeling for her has become so all-penetrating and all-diffused as to be unrecognisable. One of the most profoundly pessimistic things ever uttered by a poet was uttered by Matthew Arnold in speaking of the divine concealment of what might conceivably be the secret of our life.

> "The guide of our dark steps a triple veil
> Between our senses and our sorrow keeps,
> Has sown with thousand passages the tale
> Of grief, and eased us with a thousand sleeps."

And this exactly answers to what I am now saying; for if we were not distracted by the thousand and one little stabs we get from her diurnal tongue how should we not realise more often that terrible possibility underlying it all that one day this soft strange earth into which our roots have sunk will be taken from us by death?

Nor is it any wonder that, as time goes on, our conscious happiness grows to be more and more dependent on the unconscious happiness of having this woman at our side.

As I have hinted a man is strangely detached from Nature; and deep in his heart lies a fear of Life beyond the comprehension of any woman.

But holding a woman by night and by day *between him and Life,* he is protected from this underlying fear. He is like a frightened infant who has got back into the snug cowry-shell of inviolable safety from which he was driven forth at the cutting of his navel-string. He is free to be happy now in all the ways most natural to him.

Although sublimely unaware of this, his proud detached thoughts can take their restorative flights, can make what I have pedantically called his Ichthian and Panergic acts of resistance to misery, in beautiful freedom from the assaults of the Fear of Life which so troubled his solitary youthful days. And all that he endures from her sharp tongue is an essential part of his protection! He will say, "Life is more real to me now. It was only half-real before." And what he means is that the fear of Life which dogged his bachelor steps with unspeakable horrors, just because of his mental detachment from Nature, has now been warded off from him in some inscrutable way.

He thinks to himself, "I was lured on by her satiny limbs to take this creature to my bosom; and now I am scourged by her serpent tongue and sucked down alive into her Lamia-maw," but even while such thoughts cross his mind he finds it pleasanter, easier, more natural to him to think his proud thoughts, to live in his proud secret world, than it was before he met her.

And this is because he is no longer face to face in his helpless masculine detachment, with the chaotic ocean of Life.

That satiny body, those tender ways, that terrible tongue, are now between him and Life. And his protection is the more assured because this Being who now lies between him and Nature is herself a microcosm of Nature, armed with Nature's cruellest claws, as well as dowered with her most magical allurements.

Our "Pilgrim and Sojourner" is therefore free to think his sublime thoughts, and nourish his moral pride, and indulge his moral scruples, and practise —as long as it does not mean giving away money— his ascetic ideals; but he is only free to do this in the large magnanimous leisure of his liberated soul because between him and Nature there is now *another Nature,* because between him and the Battle of Life there is now a Battalion of Belligerency, ten times more courageous than he is.

But all this advantage to the man in question is not attained without loss to someone. One of the wickedest laws of Nature seems to be that it is hard for one soul to gain even a spiritual advantage without some measure of loss incurred by another.

And who are they who pay the price of this new freedom for the man to assert himself and realise his identity? They are his friends! Nothing is more noticeable than the way a man's personality and his glowing conceit of it grow and increase after he has lived for some time with his woman. She may attack him fiercely when they are alone, but in relation to the external world—especially in relation to his

friends—she pumps pride into him from a bound-
less ocean of magnetic sympathy till he acquires a
power to assert his humours, his opinions, his tastes,
that sometimes becomes preposterous.

And his old cronies don't know what to make of
it; and even his family learn at last to treat him
with becoming respect. He was airily egoistic before, but now his friends find his egoism a much
graver, heavier and more solidly rooted thing. He
had his happy and unhappy moods before, but now
he seems to assert his personality from the hidden
ground of some reserve of force that renders him,
not pompous perhaps, but inviolably assured.

All his little personal ways and peculiarities, all
his quirks and his crotchets, seem to have received
some sort of authoritative seal that renders them
sacred; and whereas before he had to take the world
as it came, the world has now to take *him* as he
comes.

Aspects of his nature that he had never dared to
display before he now not only boldly displays but
obviously glories in. It is as if he walked and talked
from above the support of an invisible body beneath him. And there *is* an invisible body beneath
him. Under him is the everlasting lap! His mental
pride in his opinions, that profound and perpetual
cause of happiness to him, is doubled. And yet these
are the very opinions that daily melt into thin air

under the touch of the realistic tongue at his side.

His friends can no longer afford to treat him in the old way as a half-man, to be made little of, to be pushed casually about, to be fooled and disregarded and laughed at. "There is no arguing with him," they say. "He is changed. He thinks he is Someone now. She has spoiled him."

But what in reality has happened is this. For the first time in his life the poor man has been given the privilege to round off his personality to its full circle. With her between him and the great outer chaos he has been allowed to circle at leisure on his orbit until he has taken to himself the form of a round opaque impregnable world.

It was a woman who gave him his first birth. It is a woman who has given him his second birth. He is now a twice-born man.

In conclusion let me say this. What any man, finding his life difficult with a woman, were wise to do, if he cares for his happiness or hers, is to use to the limit all the measure of moral pride that Nature has given him. Let him put aside all spiritual experiments in humility, whether Christian or otherwise, till the waters are less stormy. What the waves need just now is the oil of his masculine pride of self-control!

For, whatever happens, he must never under any

circumstances get angry with her. It is true that his anger is what, consciously or unconsciously, she longs to excite, and it is true that if the explosion did come there might possibly follow a warm and tearful reconciliation; but what she gains in this, and what they both gain in the resultant reconciliation, are not worth the risk of his giving up the particular thing in his deepest soul that in the long run establishes their happiness on its firmest foundation.

The reader must remember that this book is concerned with the technique of human happiness rather than with the problem of how to be nobler and more spiritual than we are; and what I feel is, that in the creation of such a technique while it is necessary to take many weapons from the armoury of God, it is also necessary to take a few from the armoury of the Devil. In other words if you want to be happy with a girl you must, at the very bottom of your soul, reconcile your conscience to be being both good and bad.

The moral unction in a man that helps him to keep his temper and answer gently when his woman is scolding is not a wholly noble thing. It is an ambiguous quincunx, compounded of one part pity, one part reason, and three parts pride.

But such as it is, it is in harmony with his nature just as for her to give full rein to her anger and full rein to her love, is in harmony with hers.

Secretly they will often both yearn to change each other's nature or to get back to that mystical fusion which existed, or at least which they imagined existed, when they were first in love; and, of the twain, I think it is usually the woman who makes the most violent efforts to change the inmost identity of the other. But it is all wrong! The whole meaning, interest, and reward, the whole glory and tragedy of their association, is now that he should be a man to the limit, and that she should be a woman to the limit, but a man and a woman whose happiness is forever being renewed by the building of eternally new bridges over an everlasting gulf.

WORKS AND DAYS

I WOULD LIKE THIS LITTLE BOOK ON THE ART OF Happiness to be of such a nature that its main gist could be understood by a person who existed three thousand years ago and also by a person who will exist three thousand years hence; nor is this a fantastic or presumptuous desire.

It is a legitimate philosophic implication, a hope that I have, for good or ill, got down to some eternal recurrence in our human situation.

Consider for example a line that with trifling modifications returns again and again throughout Homer's Odyssey,

"Asmenoi ek thanatoio, philous olesantes hetairous."
"Glad to have escaped death, though we had lost
    our dear companions."

Now this simple and deep sigh of relief is expressive of what should be, and what generally is,
apart from some morbid twist of the mind in the
direction of despairing futility, the natural resilience
of the vital principle at the bottom of our being.

Not to be dead yet, not to be quite dead yet, is
our ultimate human cause of self-congratulatory
satisfaction. The irrevocable blow has fallen upon
someone near and dear to us, is at this moment fall-
ing upon many of our human brothers and sisters,
but we, "protero pleomen," we have "sailed on,"
still prepared to wrestle with life, still prepared to
make that fierce "in-spite-of-all" act of the defiant
mind.

Well then, what interests me now is to wonder
and speculate as to what the mental attitude of a
person will be three thousand years hence. Will
people, under conditions totally beyond our present
imagination, when scientific inventions and social
adjustments have rendered the life-struggle incon-
ceivably easier than it is to-day, still think of their
personal happiness as important, still feel "asmenoi
ek thanatoio, philous olesantes hetairous," "glad to
have escaped death though they have lost their dear
companions?"

Or will they have acquired some totally new mental attitude in which personal "gladness" has become negligible?

It is hard for me to believe in this latter possibility. It is hard for me to believe that, even after three thousand years of scientific experiments and three thousand years of communistic or anarchistic re-adjustments, the basic urge of a living personal soul will be different from what it is to-day and what is was in Homer's time. The more intense communal consciousness of our western world at the present hour, combined with the industrial fashion that we name "mass-production" and combined too with the modern tendency to nationalistic dictatorship is just at present charging our psychic atmosphere with social *as against individual life-consciousness.*

But it seems to me that it would be a great psychological blunder to regard the present disintegration of the old stoical cults of the individual mind confronting the Cosmos as something final.

"Everything," as Heraclitus says, "flows away," except the battle of the Everlasting Opposites, and among these warring opposites no battle is more deep-rooted than that between the individual and all that hinders his self-realisation.

There is a feeling among us to-day, a feeling that runs like hypnotic electricity from person to person, that since the Universe is totally without purpose, totally without meaning, totally without guidance, totally without reason, or justice, or mercy, or pity, and with absolutely nothing left but the hugger-mugger, hurly-burly, ramshackle beauty of litter and chance and chaos, there is no cause why we should take anything seriously, make any effort to philosophise seriously about anything; but every cause why we should drift along recklessly and carelessly, always jesting, always unhappy, always ironically simple and simply ironical, not grandiloquently bitter in the old solemn, Satanic way, but puckishly indifferent, too indifferent to be anything but humorous and harmless, despairing and well-meaning, addicted to drink but averse to crime, and for all our mania for bagatelles really more well-behaved *than the universe deserves.*

It will be doubtless from this particular kind of airy despair, less witty and more chaotic than the elegant futility before the French Revolution, that our time will receive its especial spiritual stamp among the ages, and there will very likely always be individual souls who will return to this, just as there will always be some who will return to the Middle Ages and some who will return to the Classic world.

But whatever the peculiar value of this age of spiritual futility and de-personalised despair may be, it cannot be regarded as an age from which a philosopher of happiness can draw much help for his technique. He must however at least make sure that the chemicals he uses for his mental soap-bubbles contain enough of the authentic rainbow tints of human happiness to survive the critical air of this ambiguous time.

It is interesting to speculate upon a possible History of Human Happiness that would indicate at what particular epochs the individual suffered most and was—apart from famine, pestilence, and war—most unhappy.

I think the Puritan Age, particularly in its effect on women and children, must have been a thousand times more deadly to our natural gladness in "sailing on, still alive, though we have lost our dear companions," than this age of our own, with its cult of de-personalised futility. It is better to jest under the empty eye-sockets of Nothingness than to weep and howl under the blood-sucking glare of Jehovah.

And this brings us to the crucial question as to whether it were wise to introduce religion at all into such a basic technique of happiness as ours.

I may be a Stone-Worshipper and you may be an Icon-Worshipper; for the purposes of this book it will, I think, be an advantage to pretend, both of us, to be advocates of a dogmatic materialistic athe-

ism. Such a pretence will not be altogether easy; for
we are so involved with our own past and with the
long past of our race that it is a struggle to free our
minds, even yet, from all idea of some intelligent
purpose in the universe; but since there are many
men and women who *have* thus freed their minds,
even though to the rest their freedom may seem a
desolate and fanatical laceration, I am anxious to
make my present technique such an inclusive system
that it can appeal to the most austere rejector of
religious drugs.

Well then, as Whitman would say, "whoever you
are," think of yourself as absolutely alone in an unfathomable universe. As to these other selves, these
people of your most intimate life, you will have to
make them also part and parcel of this blind, pur-
poseless, godless chaos that surrounds you on every
side.

And over what, in this terrifying welter of alien
things, have you got control? Over one thing alone,
over yourself! This is the power of which Socrates
made so much, and of which millions of "superior
men" in China still make so much. This is the
philosophy underlying that rather tiresome "cheerio!"
attitude of so many average Englishmen.

And after all it is the deepest religious act possible to the soul of man. It is in fact the worship of
Life itself, whereof the eternal Litany is,

"Though thou tormentest me, yet will I rejoice in thee!"

But granting we have established this basic point in our technique, granting that we have suggested the wisest procedure in the problem of sex-relationship, the next step is to suggest the craftiest method of making use of the little daily relaxations and pleasures that intersperse our life's work. Nature comes first among these, and the great point in regard to our interest in Nature is that it should not be confined to her more grandiose and startling phenomena but concentrated upon those aspects of her appearance which are attainable by us all and familiar to us all.

Among these appearances I would put first the traditional Four Elements. These are those mysterious presences that it is better as far as our happiness is concerned to regard, as Spengler says Goethe did, with the *physiognomic eye,* the eye through which they reveal themselves to our senses, rather than with the scientific eye, the eye through which they appear as electronic vibrations.

We ought to be always on the look-out for some sort of living substitutes for that religious awe in the presence of life which our race has cultivated so long. To cut down on the religious sense in the wholesale manner advocated by Lucretius seems a sorry neglect of a natural, if monstrously perverted, instinct. And our attitude to the four great elements, to the earth, to the divine ether, to the sea and all the waters, to the sun and the moon and all the stellar bodies, to the wind and to the rain and the frost and the dew, to the motions of the clouds and the processions of the seasons, to darkness itself as it mingles with the mystery of the two twilights, ought to be an attitude containing all the actual feelings implied in the word "worship," ought to be, in fact, a real substitute for religion, the only substitute perhaps, except an inspired pity for flesh and blood, that the scepticisms of our age allow us.

And second to this feeling for the primal elements, this response to every aspect of earth and sun and wind and water that filters through to us between the crevices of our practical concerns, I think by far our most important awareness is the indescribable thrill that comes to us from certain chance effects of the spectacle of life, certain casual groupings of people and things, not necessarily beautiful at all but giving to our existence a sudden magical heightening.

With this heightening there often comes the strange feeling that we have been stirred by these very things in some other, different life. This may well be an illusion and the thrilling happiness we feel may be simply a stirred-up memory of the experiences of our early years.

But whatever this subtle emotion may be, it is

something that "redeems all sorrows" and brings us a wondrous moment of *recognition*, as if, though pilgrims from far away, we have followed this road before.

But I would like to give a few more concrete details of these evasive feelings that I regard as so important.

One sensation that I always feel to be especially fraught with this emotion is the curious *metallic whiteness* of water just before nightfall. There is something about this particular whiteness that suggests all the mystic recoveries that have ever been, from all the lost battles and all the lost causes that have ever been, in the long procession of men's lives.

Another phenomenon that I always feel stirs up something "rich and strange" in the depths of our soul is the particular look of any ancient time-worn object that is associated with humanity when caught against a wide-stretching background. This might be a post, or a group of posts for instance washed by water and standing with its long mystic endurance against some receding sky-line, or water-line, or horizon-line, that draws our spirit towards the infinite. Of the nature of such an infinite this old worm-eaten object, this old post it may be, comes to partake in an unconscious affinity of congruity; those elements "that themselves are old" answering

to the character of this forlorn Inanimate and forever summoning it to share their immunity from
annihilation.

Another casual sight within the scope of everyone
and full of a singular power of stirring the imagination is any fragment of roof-top or wall-coping
when you catch it in the yellow light of the rising or
descending sun. Thus transfigured, the mere fact
of the thing resting there, in its immobility, with the
immense gulfs of air sinking away into illimitable
space behind it, evokes, as it lies back upon the
calm mystery of dawn or of evening, the feeling
that it is the golden threshold of some land of
enchantment into which our soul can enter and find
a solution of all the paradoxes of life.

There are a thousand other such things in the
dreariest neighbourhood; only we cannot catch their
secret until we have learned to ask from Nature,
not so much beauty or picturesqueness, as a certain
poetic *suggestiveness* that can start our mind on a
long vista of vague brooding.

Yet another aspect of Nature *where the familiar
suddenly becomes unfamiliar*—which is the chief
cause of those sudden unaccountable waves of happiness that carry us on such strange voyages towards
the receding shores of the land of heart's desire—is
the sight of a single wide-stretching branch of a dis-
tant tree, that, as we gaze on it, seems to be floating

on a mystic sea of air, of air so liquid, so trans-
parent, so far-receding, that it is as if the branch
that rests upon it were drawing to itself, out of that
immensity, the very secret of life and death. I say
"of life and death," for those who wish to know
what real happiness is before they die will do well
to make the utmost of that feeling that comes upon
us all sometimes, it may be in the presence of the
faintest weft of rose-tinged vapour floating in the
West when all the rest of the sky is dark, or it may
be from some other omen of the way, a feeling as
if we were on the very verge of bringing life and
death so close to each other that they flow together
and mingle, and as if the terror of death, no longer
isolated, would in another minute be transmuted
into *something else.*

What we feel at these times is more significant
than any occasion for our feeling, but it is also
something that it is easy enough to discount in our
cynical moods.

What it seems to carry with it, this deep recurrent feeling, so closely connected with all manner of
transitory effects of light and darkness, is an instinct
that life and death are not absolute opposites but
are fatally involved with each other; are indeed the
double-edged manifestation of some *third thing*
beyond the power of our reasoning to conceive.

At the bottom of all lasting happiness is an accumulative reservoir of these particular moments, and their value is proved by the fact that when we recall any long epoch of our past the worries and discomforts sink quite out of sight, and certain floating impressions of an evasive sensuous character remain, as if they were the essence of all those years! And they *are* the essence of those years and of all the years of our life, and if there is any planetary memory in our ancient earth, storing up, long after we are dead, what we have felt, these moments will be the abiding essence of that too, our individual contribution to the tellurian consciousness! The thing to do is to use your will to force the passing moment to become a medium for the eternal.

Never compare the present with the past. Never anticipate the future. Pull yourself up the second you begin pitying yourself for being *here* rather than *there*.

Too much has been made of hope. The better a philosopher you are the less will you hope. To hope is the most unphilosophical of all mental acts, for it implies that you are failing in the supreme achievement of turning the present into the eternal.

"Hope deferred maketh the heart sick." To the devil with it then!

And instead of calling up imaginary changes in your life or hoping for this or that, the moment you have any time for awareness, the second you are able to look round you and take stock of things, make a resolute effort to convert what you see, be it the dreariest collection of objects, into what has *some* poetic significance. The great thing is to cultivate the power of obliterating what displeases you among these objects and of *making it invisible,* and then of concentrating on what has some kind of remote appeal to your imagination, if not to your senses.

Force these objects round you, however alien, to yield to your defiant resolve to assert yourself through them and against them. Get hold of the moment by the throat. Do not submit to the weakness of waiting for a change. *Create a change* by calling up the spiritual force from the depths of your being. This is an attitude of mind that you can turn into an automatic habit by doing it again and again. Rape the moment as it passes. It can never pass again; and for all you know its very drabness may prove a loop-hole into the eternal if you press against it hard enough.

Never wait for the future; never regret the past; make the present serve as past and future together. And if the moment is one of complete misery, lift up your head still, as even the wicked Macbeth had the heart to do, and say to yourself, "Though Birnam Wood *be* come to Dunsinane and *thou* opposed—"

But suppose you are watching the rain-drops on your window, or the straight line of a roof against a grey sky, or a wavering column of ascending smoke, or the edge of a dark cloud tinged with fire, or a sea-groin patched with green seaweed, or rooks following a plough, the pleasure you can get from these simple things is not entirely simple, as you force yourself to isolate and enjoy their poetic significance. For with this moment of your feeling there mingles the feeling of all your fathers before you, they who in their day and hour looked at the same things.

It is true that what, in the past of all your progenitors' lives, you are fusing with the pressure of your immediate present is no definite thing, no series of definite things. It is only a vague sense that the feeling of life which you are now experiencing in this moment of detachment from your activity is rich with the memories of all the generations behind you.

The streams of all our lives' consciousness run with a double flow, the salt water of action and the fresh water of contemplation, and no man's days are complete without an awareness of both. Fortunate is the man who, when he is at rest for a single second, indoors or out, in the course of his day's experience possesses the power of sinking back, back and away from the pressure of his immediate concern, and of gazing calmly at whatever surrounds him, however grotesque and unappealing it may be, and of saying to himself, "Well! Here am I, a living consciousness still, and there is *that;* and by simply looking at *that* and isolating myself with *that,* and using *that* as the temporary, casual, accidental, incongruous *surrounding of my undefeated spirit,* I lift *that* with me, for this single unassailable moment, into another dimension, lift it with me, for all its grotesqueness, and set it among the eternal things in the memory of the cosmic consciousness!"

This momentary sinking away from the whole world of action into a complete relaxation of body and mind, and into an hypnotic stare upon any little object within sight, can become, when you set to work to cultivate it, not only an important act of awareness of the deeper life-flow, but a most comforting and healing refreshment.

For its essence is both philosophical and non-moral and because of its absolute detachment from all practical concerns it is wholly irresponsible. In that "eternal moment" the self in you faces the Not-self, making use of any little inanimate thing near you as a symbol of the whole universe.

Immersed in a thousand absorbing activities of work and play we tend to forget the continuity of our inner consciousness of life; we tend to forget our absolute and *cumulative* loneliness. These "eternal moments" of lying back upon the soul, and of letting ourselves become nothing but pure awareness, nothing but a conscious mind face-to-face with any fragment of the inanimate that happens to be near us, are moments which, if we want to be happy and to live long, we ought to snatch from the flowing of time. Snatch them in busses, in waitingrooms, in railway-trains, on park-seats, in hall-ways, in the entrances of hotels and theatres, in public lavatories, on ferry-boats, in taxis, in carriers' carts, in churches, on your bed, on a chair in your kitchen, on the steps of your house, over the fence of your garden; snatch them whenever and wherever you can!

The essence of these moments is that you sink down for a perceptible breathing-space into absolute *irresponsibility*.

This is the only way to be increasingly happy, and the only way to save our nerves from being worn out. Infants have this power, and very old people have it; and we are throwing away the Nectar of Life when we refuse, in the heat of the day, to reproduce the beatitude of its beginning and its end.

You will find it advisable to conceal from your friends these daily immersions into the Sacred Fount of Irresponsibility. Nothing is more irritating to a companion, all agitated and wrought up over some transitory mishap or some threatening crisis, than to catch you thus floating at ease, detached in this deep underflow of the world; but if you refuse to culti-vate this divine secret, woe to your happiness in life!

What you really do in these moments of heavenly irresponsibility is not only deliberately to assert the blessed privilege of infancy and old age, but at once to revert to some vegetation-epoch of the past and to anticipate some godlike condition of the future. The technique of any real happiness has much more to do with what is absurdly called a person's hum-drum, work-a-day life, than with the great crises of his days. But all these phrases such as work-a-day, hum-drum, commonplace, ordinary, dull, monotonous, are words invented by silly and frivolous weaklings.

Life is life; and it is the business of the individual to be happy in *life itself,* not to require perpetual *bonnes bouches* from fate, and gala-days from chance, and grand high festivals from destiny.

But the great trick is to make it your deepest re-ligion and your starkest morality to force yourself to be happy and to concentrate yourself on growing steadily happier. The whole secret lies in this con-tinuity of stoical habit; and if you aim at it con-stantly you will find that you begin to take a grim satisfaction in the harsh occasions when your philosophy is put to the test.

And when the important question arises how far you are wise, in regard to your permanent happiness, to sacrifice pleasure to culture, it is this necessity of continuity and growth that has to be specially considered. The best way is to compromise. There are certain universal pleasures like going to the movies, like reading the daily papers, or absorbing yourself in melodramatic fiction, that are so sweet and delicious to our common human nature that it would seem absurd to give them up.

But it is a still greater mistake to have no other relaxation-string or contemplative-string to the bow of our happiness than these popular distractions.

What everyone needs is some irresponsible undertaking that is at once capable of infinite development and has nothing to do with our regular life's-work or with public success in the world. Some substitute for what we English call a "Hobby" is what *all* human beings require. An "Untouchable" in Calcutta, a beggar in Benares, a gypsy in New York, a composer of fiction for the mob in London, a retired gentleman in Dorset, an emancipated Hareem-Queen in Istanbul, we all, if we are to enjoy any *continuity of happiness,* must hit upon some queer personal enterprise, if it be only watching dung-beetles, or learning Latin, or collecting

— 219 —

fossils, or playing the Jews' Harp, or making patch-
work quilts, or cutting walking-sticks, or studying
botany, or adding to our ancestral songs and legends,
the mere thought of which, when we wake in the
morning, gives us that peculiar glow which only a
love-affair or a person's private secret play-passion is
able to evoke.

The whole art of happiness is rooted and
grounded in two things, *in will-power and in routine.* If I annoy you by saying this you must remember that I am talking about the "art" of this thing.
Some airy-winged waftures of voyaging happiness
come to us all, independent of any philosophical
methods, but what this book is concerned with is
technique alone, technique whether moral or im-
moral, whether hard or easy.

All happiness depends on a *certain quantity of
something and no more;* and it is to limit ourselves
to this "certain quantity"—and not to go on indulging in the thing till it smells like a blown-out candle
in a chilly dawn—that we have to use our will.

If you have a mania for cigarettes for instance
you ought always to postpone your "next" till you
have read so much, or written so much, or walked
so far, or looked at the clock for so long. You are
deliberately murdering the enchanted Houris of sensual delight that live in cigarette-smoke when you
let yourself smoke as much as you feel inclined

without any sort of restraint. And every time you put off your "next" the least little longer you are increasing not only your pleasure in smoking but your happiness in life.

A person who smokes *sans cesse* reduces himself to the level of a person who doesn't smoke at all; indeed he becomes like those who take warmth and food and shelter *for granted,* which is a blasphemy against your whole life upon earth, and is the chief reason why the rich man finds it so hard to enter the "kingdom."

But returning to the crucial question of pleasure *versus* culture; as I hinted above the best thing to do is to compromise. To give up the absorbed delight that a man takes in his daily paper and that a woman takes in her story-book because there exist vistas of more intellectual satisfaction in other things seems a self-denying ordinance that goes too far. It is better to think deep "asides" while we read superficialities, than to think superficial "asides" while we read profundities! It is what goes on in the mind that matters.

There is no better example of the solemn hypocrisy of most of us men than the grave manner in which we read our newspaper, furtively revelling in the murders and the advertisements, but assuming the air of so many Mr. Gladstones pondering over high affairs of State. So hypnotic is our moral gravity that we have got it firmly established that a man reading his paper is a sacred sight in the eyes of God, whereas a woman reading her novel is quite a different matter.

But sacred or frivolous, pious or impious, these heavenly oases of irresponsibility when we lose ourselves in the honeyed anonymity of "A Person Reading," ought not to be rejected. These divine interludes are like Blessed Interments to our tired bodies, like Heavenly Requiems to our fevered souls. We rest, we forget, and for a while are happy.

An epicure in newspaper-reading naturally fights shy of evening papers unless he has no time to read the morning one; and, except out of consideration for those who sell them, it seems as as if to purchase the morning's news at midnight were like assisting at a ghastly premature birth.

As far as his solid happiness goes I think that a passion for fiction-reading, so good for a girl, is bad for a young man. A young man's neurotic detachment from Reality makes fiction for him—unless it be attended by an intellectual effort—a perilous and disintegrating drug; whereas for a girl, whose life is already more immersed in Reality than her nerves can bear, the reading of fiction is a legitimate escape into that inner world of reverie and brooding fancy which ought, *all her life long,* to be the undertide of her soul's existence.

A young man is already so much in himself "a
work of fiction" that if he gets a mania for second-
rate or third-rate novels he will lose what power he
already possesses for polishing up his weapons of
attack and defence in his struggle with life.

But thrice-blessed are these writers of fiction,
first-rate as well as fifth-rate, that can so ensorcerize
a woman that for a while she can forget this accursed Reality to which every fibre in her being so
fatally responds!

There is nothing in Nature, except swallows dip-
ping into a stream, so eminently harmonious as the
sight of a woman lost in a book; and the best thing
every girl can possibly do for her happiness in life
is to acquire as soon as possible, and indulge to the
limit, a passion for fiction-reading.

Such fiction can never corrupt her taste or hurt
her culture, because in the pedantic, aesthetic, and
philosophical sense she does not give herself up to
it or "take it hard" as a man would do. I do not
mean that she tosses the "style" and the "philosophy" aside, as she would toss aside the supere-
rogatory portions of a man's conversation, for she has
no philosophical conceit, rendering her supercilious
to her author's musings; but what really concerns her
are the characters and the plot, and upon these—and
with some justification—she concentrates, and lets
the rest go by.

The truth is that women are so much more porous

to what you might call *unofficial culture* than men that it does not hurt them to read things that cannot be called classical; nor does such reading hinder the growth of their originality.

But with men it is totally different. When "successful" men begin, as they often do—and it is a sure sign of the peculiar degeneracy that comes from "success"—to read the worthless trash that alone amuses them, and to be supercilious to any poor devil they catch trying to improve his mind, what they are doing is displaying a dangerous contempt for that "good of the intellect" without which, according to Dante, our end must be Hell.

When a successful man relaxes his enterprising intelligence over a detective-story he resembles a monkey gravely pre-occupied in catching lice; whereas when a hard-working woman snatches a moment to absorb herself in a second-rate romance it is as if she were indulging in some restorative, fecund, vegetative process, like that of a cow chewing the cud.

However this may be, there is no doubt that our daily happiness is immeasurably heightened by the undertaking of some intellectual task totally dissociated from our work. The advantage for instance to be got from the slow acquiring of a foreign language, and the gradual mastery, be it of only *one* single favourite classic, is of incalculable value.

But for this sort of thing it is imperative that a person should choose a really great book, a book saturated with the essential tragedy and comedy of things, the same thousands of years ago as to-day.

And at this point it is worth pausing to note that the books which permanently add to a person's mellowest wisdom are not the startling intellectual works that bring us a new and exciting *aperçu* upon life, but the old humanistic works that carry with them the sort of massive, simple, epicurean stoicism that reduces to a few large noble outlines the chaotic pell-mell of our existence.

It certainly does not require any exceptionable linguistic aptitude to make use of a laconic phrase such as "aequam memento rebus in arduis servare mentem" when your worries thicken about you; and verses like these—the sublime commonplace of good sense—are not the worse for having been mixed with the ups and downs of human life for a few thousand years.

And now we arrive at the crucial problem of the effect, upon the over-tones and under-tones of our life, of our actual daily work.

All our days must of necessity be in a large part days of action; and the spirit in which we carry through this diurnal labour counts for more than the nature of the labour itself.

It is all relative. The most miserably incompetent human being can derive a certain degree of satisfaction from an uncongenial job, if he accepts it without too much self-pity and makes the utmost of every little advance in efficiency he can compass.

The best mental trick is to think of jobs that are *worse* than our own, rather than of those that are more agreeable; and if our job *is* really the worst possible to us and devoid of the least grain of compensation, there still remains our dogged reserve of will-power to keep us going till the accursed hours have come to an end.

We can, so to speak, shut our eyes and harden our heart till the moment arrives for release. "Be the day weary, be the day long, at length it ringeth to evensong"; and the Devil himself must be in it if, when our daily release comes, we cannot relax our senses in a paradisiac felicity, quite unknown to the lucky workers whose jobs have *some* dregs of interest! Many victims of this sort because of their resentment at what our economic system has done to them, naturally turn communist.

The Communistic Credo seems to have something of that psychic power of objectifying personal sufferings in an outward historic movement that the worship of a God of Suffering was wont in former times to possess, but the average man who is at the end of his tether is as a rule more prone to "eat his

own heart," as Homer says, in solitary despair, than
to sink his individual wretchedness in either the Religion of the Proletariat or that of the Man of
Sorrows.

It does indeed remain a sardonic commentary
upon the social arrangements of our mortal life that
into so many hearts the Iron has sunk so deep that
for a writer to discuss happiness at all seems a
ghastly joke.

With regard to this joke Christ still has something
to say, and Communism still has something to say,
while an honest philosopher—like Marcus Aurelius
in his imperial seat at the Gladiatorial Circus—when
he beholds certain things can only hold his tongue.

There is such an experience however, as being
shamed into happiness, shamed out of one's silly
manias, shamed out of one's fastidiousness, shamed
out of one's querulousness, by the thought of what
some human creatures, not less sensitive than oneself, have to endure. This is no complacent satisfaction at being more lucky; it is the acquiring of what
might be called a *tragic sense of proportion.*

But I must approach now a very ticklish part of
my subject. Our power of enduring life without
breaking down is made a more formidable thing
when we throw into it a little of the "bad" in us as
well as of the "good."

And the reason for this goes deep. Our evolutionary growth, through unthinkable ages, into the sensitized ego we now are, has implied all the way down
the centuries a desperate struggle between the self
and the not-self. Into this struggle the endless semi-
conscious "selves" of the lower organisms flung
their whole life-force, a force including much of
what to our further developed moral sense appears
"bad."

And into this reservoir of "bad," into this
"Old Adam," as the Bible calls it, of our lonely
fighting-for-our-own-hand, it is necessary to lower
our spiritual buckets now and again, cautiously so
and reservedly so, but still shamelessly and boldly,
if we are to nourish our happiness upon its natural
sustenance.

That is the whole point. By reason of some mysterious urge from the mystery behind Nature we
are developing, in pain and grief, a conscience so
sensitive and withal so easily perverted—that it
takes very little to turn it into an intermittent torment destroying all chance of steady happiness.

I do not mean that we must be violent or ruthless
or greedy or cruel in order to be happy; but there
are elements of the "bad" in us that we have got
boldly to make use of, if we are anxious not to slip
into hopeless nervous misery.

It is a curious thing, for instance, that men at any

rate, feel more spirit and courage to deal with the shocks and discomforts of life when they are stirred by erotic lust.

And this leads me to a further and a more subtle point. What we call sadism is one of the worst forms of evil in the world and any actual practise of it is an abominable crime; and yet I am almost tempted to suggest that the only way in which the First Cause manages to endure the spectacle of the universe is by means of a certain modicum of what you might call *diffused sadism. Our* "diffused sadism," as we face the blood-stained arena of life, can afford to be much more diluted with pity than that of the First Cause; but it does remain that there is a certain battle-lust, a certain Mars-and-Venus mood of sublimated erotic energy, that gives us courage to face the Jungle of the World without being rendered too unhappy.

To call up this mood, as far as men are concerned —and I daresay in the case of women too—it is necessary deliberately to make the most of our natural attraction to the opposite sex. It seems ridiculous to leave to the bold bad unscrupulous people all the old reckless love-making spirit that has so often made timorous souls grave.

Let "men of good will" exploit at least enough of this dare-deviltry of the "bad" to get what you might call the recklessness of Nature on their side.

Nietzsche goes too far with his "blond-beast" talk; but an ounce of the sexual urge makes us braver than the "logoi" of many sages.

Yes, if we are honest with ourselves we must admit that there is no escape from the necessity of being deliberately, consciously, and wilfully "bad" as well as "good."

We must leave to Saints and to the few real Christians left, the desperate privilege of aiming only at being good.

And there is something else necessary too, and whether you regard this as good or bad will depend on your particular philosophy. We must, if we are to have any secure happiness in this world, and this cannot be emphasized too often for all depends on it, realise what might be called our cosmic loneliness in Time and Space. We must habitually think of ourselves as complete strangers to this earth, strangers who have been flung into life and have been given a father and mother and brothers and sisters and a mate and children and boy-friends and girl-friends, but *strangers* from the beginning to the end.

And if on the strength of this ultimate feeling of loneliness we can manage to cultivate the power of looking at our daily companions, at our mate, at our parent, at our child, at our brother or sister, and of saying to ourself, "So *you* are the Image, *you* are the Mask, that I have been catapulted against from out of the infinite unknown!" it will be better for them and for us too. For in this way, by the obliteration of superficial grievances, we shall feel a great wave of pity surging up within us—"You too," we shall think, "you *other* strangers from the Unknown, you too are 'pestered in this pinfold here.' "

And since both of us are what they call *landed,* let us be as decent to each other as we can and for as long as we can!

I don't think men who are unhappy in their life with their women suffer anything like the misery that women do who are unhappy with their men, but I think an unmarried girl living with her parents is the creature who suffers most *from fellow-creatures* in the whole world.

These sufferings—the sufferings of the unmarried daughter—are far worse in England than in America; in fact they are so cruel that if this impious little book has the effect of helping any young woman in England to endure her life with her parents it would completely justify its existence.

What a pity that Shakespeare did not live to write a sequel to King Lear, in which some noble daughter of Edgar or Albany were hounded to death in a tragic attempt to rebel against her righteous father!

It is far more difficult in these days, though it is easier in America than in England, for a girl to assert herself against her mother, than against her father, but great external Revolutions in History imply less spiritual rending and tearing and emotional bloodshed than are implied in these intimate insurrections.

I expect one cause of unhappiness in the lives of all of us are those tremendous commandments, in both the Old and the New Testament, commanding us to love, instead of commanding us to be at peace in our own soul. When you think of the piteous and lamentable attempts young people have made *to love perforce* it makes you realise that any honest Hand-book of Happiness must strike its operating knife to the heart of this ambiguous doctrine.

What a liberating flood of planetary happiness pours through us when we experience that great moment of Conversion, turning us from love to peace! It is then that we realise that we can be free and happy and honourable and pitiful and kind *and yet not have to love anybody.*

The great thing is to sink so deep into your individual loneliness that you can look at every single person in your life and say to yourself, "Oh, so *that's* you, is it? Well, *you* didn't ask to be born any more than I asked to be born. Let us therefore be

indulgent and tender to each other to the limit; and
as for that Starlight and Nothingness that they call
love—"

Certainly we owe an incalculable debt to Freud
and his followers in ridding us of the vicious idealism of the Christian idea that sensual pleasure is
wicked; but this does not mean that we need spoil
the romance of our erotic life by accepting all the
Freudian catch words. We human beings suffer so
miserably, both in our daily work and in our passive
moments, because we represent a transitional period
—God knows it is a long enough period!—between
the happy half-consciousness of animals and the full
self-consciousness of the super-men of the future.

In this transitional epoch our minds are conscious,
but we have not trained ourselves to regulate the
thoughts *of which* they are conscious. We resemble
therefore conscious automata; and this resemblance
is increased by the accursed false philosophy of the
age from which we are only now just emerging, the
bastard philosophy of behaviouristic determinism,
which has so grossly discredited the power of the
human soul.

But for the most incompetent worker at the most
mechanical and uninspiring job there is hope of
happiness if he can become the master of his
thoughts. For after all there is no form of work on
earth in which an unpractical person whose will is

set upon the task cannot derive *some* pleasure from *some* increased facility in what he is doing. Efficient he can probably never be. But all is relative; and, if he improves even a little, *that,* for him, is a sort of Napoleonic victory.

And, after all, Nature sees no difference, the Universe sees no difference, God, if there be a God, sees no difference, between a poor devil doing a little better in his work and Napoleon winning the Battle of Austerlitz. The mind is the mind, the supreme miracle. And the battle-field within the most anonymous non-entity, the battle-field of Mr. Nobody's weakness *versus* Mr. Nobody's will, is as important to the Universe, *if the Universe cares for anything at all,* as the greatest outward event ever recorded.

And when it comes to the matter of happiness in your work, the grand trick is to "make the fig" at your employer, "make the fig" at your own advancement, and just enjoy with proud satisfaction your own private victories under the eyes of that great Taskmaster, yourself.

But you must be a wise taskmaster and never forget that you work to live, not live to work! A true philosopher who sets eyes on an overworked shop-girl snatching a moment's release from her job in some romantic Novelette will stand in awe before such sacred abstraction and regard the place where she turns those enchanted pages as holy ground. In the presence of such a triumph of the mind over matter he will think in his heart "Culture may go hang! This girl is within the gates of Paradise!"

A story is a story; and in the poorest story there are airy bridges by which a human soul—for all we know an immortal soul—wins a release from Reality.

Potentially all Shakespeare and all Dostoievsky lie like pressed rose-leaves between the pages of the simplest story. The poorest tale that brings release for the imagination and oblivion from responsibility is nearer the secret of the universe than the whole pestilent Organization for which we are labouring. *Its* best justification, its only justification, is that it enables a few living sentient minds to be free from care for a few minutes. For what else do all the great economic concerns exist, save to fill the bellies and liberate the spirits of conscious human souls?

Eulogists of efficiency as if it were an end in itself, psychologists of success, as if success could bring happiness, are the false prophets of an age that has lost the true values. There is only one "successful" person in the world and that is the person who in spite of appalling afflictions remains unconquered in the depths of his soul.

A tramp who possesses his soul in unshaken peace is a nobler product of this mysterious universe than a querulous philosopher.

— 235 —

When I said that if we were to grow steadily happier as we got older we must acquire some particular ritualistic awareness in our enjoyment of food, what I meant was not so much our natural enjoyment of palatable food, as a particular and special satisfaction in certain very simple symbolic foods, such as rolls and coffee, or bread and tea. Influenced by Walter Pater I have at various times made much of the "sacramental" aspect of these simpler ways of satisfying our hunger; but what I mean in this connection is something rather different from this.

What I feel is that our secret struggle to get our life under control and to retain an undefeated spirit requires some sort of symbolic milestones along the difficult way. Religion, with its diurnal introspections and its constant tapping of a supernatural reservoir of support, afforded this kind of mental Log-Book; but for our present purpose, since faith in these things has slipped away, some *secular ritual* becomes necessary, some simple substitute for religion that we can use as a rallying point in our struggle with our melancholy.

What better secular "Introibo ad altare" could we find than the traditional one of "breaking bread?" To this may be added the act of bending over a fire, and the moment, more inevitable still, when we put out our light and turn over on our pillow.

It seems strange that so few of us, considering the difficult and tragic hours we all have to endure, are content to drift on in so hugger-mugger and casual a fashion, refusing to make the least attempt to give an interior continuity to our days. Over external events we have slight control, but it seems a pity that what *is* within our power, a conscious continuity of some sort of philosophical life, should so often never even have been attempted when we come to die.

The point I am trying to make is that although pleasurable feelings at any given moment may be denied us, there is that which no evil situation can altogether prevent, namely our power of resistance, and of *watching ourselves resist.*

And, even while we are suffering, there is a mysterious force in the mere fact that our mind is still detached from our suffering, and watching our resistance to it. Now although at the moment there may be no gleam of happiness in our grim detachment from what we are undergoing, the mind will discover later that its capacity for happiness under difficulties has been mysteriously increased. Any trial less acute than the one we have resisted without a gleam of happiness it will be now in our power to resist with an unmistakable glow of mental satisfaction.

And we are led on from this to the real doctrine

of Epicurus—a doctrine considerably different from the attitude associated with his name—namely that the *negative element* in any wise happiness is more important than the positive element.

How it is that people don't automatically, when they are suffering, remind themselves of such horrible possibilities as death by torture or death by some especially frightful accident?

This is the real Epicurean attitude, the feeling that every moment we are not in extreme pain and those we love are not in extreme pain is precious and heavenly dispensation.

And what I mean by making our daily breaking of bread, our daily kindling of fire, our nightly sinking down on our pillow, into substitutes for the old religious symbols, is that we come to associate such acts with the long series of reliefs from suffering that make up our life. These acts become like old told-over beads binding our days together; beads that cannot always gleam with an interior radiance, but that always retain a certain power of reflecting sunlight and candlelight.

But these simple symbolic moments, these milestone-memorabilia of our struggle with life, can be made into something yet greater. The thing that murders our happiness more than anything else is *worry*, not tragic concern over matters of life and death, but simply one miserable little *worry* after another: worry over what "she said," and what "he said," and what "they *may* say," worry over the rent, over debts, over dentists, doctors, lawyers, employers, over house-repairs, dress-repairs, house-utensil repairs, over people coming that we don't want to come, and over people going that we don't want to go, over frustrations to our self-assertion, failures in our work, anxiety about health, attacks of indigestion, neuralgia, tooth-ache, ear-ache, head-ache, colds, "nerves" and so forth.

Such are the diurnal tribulations—and the list has no end—that, like flying squads of locust-demons, with horns and claws, drop on us, out of the air, and scrabble at our heart's ease.

Now I am convinced that by following both the true Epicurean and the true Stoical method, by making more of the negative art of forgetting our trials than of the positive art of adding to our felicity we can best cope with these devils. Nature and our Senses see to it that the moment *worry* is removed "the pleasure which there is in life itself" begins to flow through us again. Not quite unimpeded though! For there is still another ghastly Enemy of happiness that sometimes takes the opportunity of lifting up its horrible featureless face when the magic of life is trying to stir again—I refer to that feeling of abysmal futility, as if nothing in life were interesting or exciting, from which young people especially so often suffer. This feeling of cosmic futility—which frequently has a sexual origin—is a totally different thing from what is known as "boredom." A feeling of universal futility is a philosophical weakness, the infirmity of a noble mind, whereas to boast that you are "bored" is to betray the silly superciliousness of a fool and a snob.

Polite persons feel instinctive aversion when they hear certain foul-mouthed Anglo-Saxon words—such as that familiar one which boys delight to inscribe on walls, but which the discreet editors of the great Oxford Dictionary have thought best to exclude from the English Language—but the utterance from human lips of the words "Boring, Boredom, Bored" is a far more unworthy piece of blasphemy upon life, upon this mad Hurly-Burly that contains things so obscene, things so loathsome, things so unspeakably horrible, things so touched with infinite beauty, things so riddled with infinite disgust, things so radiant, things so transfigured, things with such livid roots going down to hell, things with such flaming wing-points scorching heaven, than any use of the worst monosyllabic ribaldry that Lady Chatterley's lover in his virtuous downrightness might feel would do his mistress good!

The people whose supercilious mouths seem moulded to utter the word "bored" resemble that

absurd Mrs. General, in the Dorrit family, with her
"prunes and prisms."

Such victims of Boredom are the flea-bite enemies of their own and of other people's happiness,
and although so frivolous they can be villainously
troublesome. You may take it as an absolute rule
that no man or woman of character ever uses the
word "bored," nor do I care to meditate on the
fate of these enemies of happiness when they reach
Dante's Inferno. "Non ragionam di lor: regarda e
passa!" is the best comment on their destiny.

Boredom? In this tragic battle for happiness,
upon which we are all engaged, there is not much
leisure for that! The thing to do when you begin
to feel overpowered by your worries is to say to
yourself, "Damn it! I'm still alive; and *some* I love
are still alive. Hell! *What then?*" And having said
this the next thing to do is fling your spirit against
the pricks. I do not mean by this against the images
that torment you. I mean against the particular
material objects that *surround* you. If you are within
four walls, fling your spirit against the iron of the
grate, against the iron of the stove, against the hard
angles and opaque surfaces of the furniture! If you
are in the open, fling your spirit against the rough
edges of masonry, against the trunks of trees,
against rocks and stones and hedges, against the
blind wind and the empty air! Do not wait for the

shapes and the chemistry of these Inanimates around you to grow beautiful or attractive. Fling your spirit *against the pricks!* Fling it against the heedless ele-ments, against the indifferent walls. This very ges-ture of the soul in its desperation is a sort of *momen-tary suicide* and the relief and release you will get from it is indescribable. It is a kind of daylight turning of your face to the wall. It is a momentary death. Death, death, death. These five letters of our alphabet are a great weight in some people's lives.

The best way to dissolve their evil-smelling smoke is to contemplate steadily the only two alternatives. Either you are totally annihilated, which is only carrying on indefinitely what often happens to you when you fall asleep; or you start fresh in another dimension. There are plenty of people who, save for the physical shock of dying, would prefer to be dead than live; and while there are life-lovers to whom this is the worst that can happen, their very interest in life keeps death in its place.

But the best way is to struggle to get it *both ways,* and to cultivate all our days a certain power Nature gives us of sinking so deep below the super-ficial distractions that we really taste something of "the pleasure which there is in life *and* death."

But it is Worry and Futility, not death, that are the two worst enemies of our peace; and whether we are actively working, or passively resting, or even trying to enjoy ourselves, these two devilish Phorkyads are always at it, scrabbling to reach the chamber of our secret delight and dig their filthy witch-nails into its heart.

And how best can this everlasting worrying over little things, alternating with this sickening sense that the whole plot of our life is futile and its whole struggle a failure, be circumvented and undermined?

By sinking down—oh, such a little way down!—below the bitter salt tide of circumstance, into the deep fresh flowing of the life-and-death flood.

This is the secret. Once get lodged in your head that there will be worries of *some* kind—not your present ones perhaps, but others no less distracting —to the end of your days; once get lodged in your head that whatever worldly successes you may have that old sense of Futility will forever be there in the background—for it is the-other-side-of-the-Moon in every mind, and is co-existent with consciousness itself, with the consciousness of the gods, if there *are* gods—and you will come to see how absurd it is to go on day after day, year after year, never realising that the tremendous drama of your being a living soul at all in this great Mystery-Play is the thing to wonder at.

You worry over these things because you take the mysterious grandeur and the dark sublimity of existence, *for granted*. You are digestion-conscious, and money-conscious, and vanity-conscious; but you refuse to be Life-Conscious.

You are always aiming at the wrong thing—you aim at getting rid of worry by worrying, and at getting rid of the futility-sense by plunging into more futility; whereas if you got into the habit of imagining yourself actually dead—as at any second you may be—you will acquire that secret irresponsibility which is the diving-board of all living joy.

The thing to do is to imagine yourself suddenly flung into life from some unthinkable distance, jerked up into life from some unthinkable Limbo. You look round, you take stock of your surroundings, of your situation. What is the worst that could happen to you? Simply to be back whence you came again!

But you will say, "It is life I suffer from, not death." No, no, it is not life that hurts you so. It is the *events* of life. It is your refusal to see the wood for the trees! Small blame to you for wishing you were dead when you are the victim of an interminable procession of devastating details. But these details are not life. The death you desire is much more like life than they are. In fact, in comparison with these things it is a part of life, the eternal *other side* of life.

What we all need, what if we possess any imagination at all we can all get, is the grand release and escape of plunging into *death-in-life*. If you were really dead these things would not be so important. Your loved ones would either die too, or they would somehow survive and struggle on. When your ailment returns, when the rent-collector knocks, when your self-esteem is outraged, when your head-ache begins again, when your day's work has been a failure, *kill yourself*. It is the best thing you can do. Kill yourself in your imagination! And then when you are dead and the coffee, or the tea, is put on the table—even if it is unpaid for—you will have the privilege of suddenly *coming to life* and doing so with a deep sigh of content.

It is incredible what a number of escapes and rescues and refuges really lie between the most miserable of us and the actual bread-line.

Here sit you, here sit your companions. You have been flung into this scene from Nothingness; and, after a succession of such scenes, it won't be the bread-line or the poor-house—in all probability— but the same Nothingness that will await you again. The curious thing is that it is not the extremely poor, living from hand to mouth, who suffer most from worry and futility, but we of the bourgeois class, who have so many refuges and barriers and railings between ourselves and starvation.

What are called practical people—and dumb

idiots they mostly are—have a way of assuring us
that if we worked a little harder we shouldn't have
time to worry. Yes, and we shouldn't have time to
live either! The Lord deliver us from the oracles of
practical people!

The thing to do is to pause often in your work
and think and imagine, and say to yourself, "Well,
it will soon be over, and I shall be sipping my tea,
and stretching my legs, and thanking fate I am not
yet in the poor-house."

A wise man or a wise woman is the person who,
if work is tiring—and *all* work, including what
Homer calls "the work of love," grows tiring sometimes—calls up to mind the few really relaxed
moments that fate allows, the cup of tea, the cup
of coffee, the glass of beer, the seat by the fire, the
bench in the sun, and above all the incredible relief
of pulling the sheet under the chin when the head
sinks on the pillow. For, when you really think of
it, the moments in all our lives when, in the midst
of our work, we suddenly get one of those unaccountable thrills of happiness that seem to arise for
no reason at all, are the moments that make life
worth living.

Well, if these good moments, for all our wily
technique, are so rare, their best substitute, and this
is within our power, are these conscious anticipa-
tions of release from toil, when we sip our coffee

or tea, and smoke in peace, or finally pull the bed-clothes over us and invoke the honey-sweet embrace of the younger sister of death.

I do not mean that in acquiring the trick of dealing with our worries by sinking into that larger aspect of things underlying their turbulent surface we should cease to take practical measures to cope with these difficulties. I mean that even *while we are dealing with them,* even while we are tinkering at them and plotting and planning to get them under control, it is good to remember that at the worst our life will "go," as the negroes say, "inching along" somehow, and the world will not come to an end.

Take what practical measures you can; but always keep in touch, underneath each pre-occupation, with that detached ether of absolute irresponsibility which is the element of real life and real death. This, it is true, is much easier for a man than a woman; but on the other hand a woman's pre-occupation with any particular worry ought to be so modified, by her being so much more involved than he is with *the whole field of worry* that this especial thing does not tower up, out of all proportion, as in the man's imagination it tends to do.

One class of worries ought summarily to be dealt

with by a drastic gesture of the mind. I refer to the good opinion of others.

It is one of the worst curses of a certain type of sensitive nature, with a mania for being liked and respected, that it should always be brooding, like the luckless Macbeth, upon the "golden opinions" of other people. But those who suffer from this must make one crushing, rending, violent motion of the mind and force themselves to face the rough, jagged bed-rock reality, namely that we are all absolutely alone, and that the only ultimate censor of our behaviour is ourself. There is an important further fact in this connection, namely that our friends are much less concerned with us, whether for good or ill, whether to our praise or to our dispraise, than we are liable to imagine.

And you will be astonished how people come to accept your stubborn independence and your indifference to what they think of you, when once you begin boldly and decisively to go your own way.

We cherish the illusion that our friends are thinking of us all the time, either in praise or dispraise, whereas we ought to know, from our own thoughts of *them,* that they are far too occupied with their own affairs to give us, for either good or ill, more than the most casual concern.

This sensitiveness to the good opinion of others, even of our nearest intimates, is one of the "last infirmities" of a noble mind, but it is also the foster-nurse of endless hypocrisies. Make one crushing, crashing, confounding motion of your mind, and appoint yourself sole judge of your own behaviour.

I do not mean by this that it is not wise to yield—if you are a man—to the practical wishes of your particular woman; but, even with her, if you are to possess your soul in peace, it is best not to base your happiness upon her opinion of you. Base your happiness upon no opinion outside your own conscience; and, as I have repeated all along, you must beget a sort of *sub-conscience,* even below that, which will tell you that there are times when it is right to be deliberately *bad,* as well as deliberately good!

Hitherto I have been dealing with the definite worries that spoil our happiness in both our active and our passive hours; but now it is necessary to face that deeper and subtler enemy, the vague feeling of futility that comes over us, taking the heart out of everything, futility in ourselves, futility in Nature, futility in life.

A Machiavellian Hand-Book like this must suggest more ways than one of dealing with the various Demons that torment us. From some of these demons it is certainly best to escape by flight, and the worst of them can only be escaped by that sort of absolute flight that resembles death, I mean the absolute obliteration from our mind of what it is madness to remember; but with regard to this Demon of Futility, though no two victims of it will use the same weapons, one desperate mode of attack, if we have enough vitality to make it, is to draw in upon ourself from our immediate surrounding, gather our spirit together, like a crouching animal about to spring, and then, like the animal when it *does* spring, to plunge with a spiritual leap forward, into the vast rondure of the Cosmos about us. Our body meanwhile, in its world-weariness, remains absolutely immobile. But our spirit "Like a child from the womb, like a ghost from the tomb" plunges into the hard resistant curves and angles and planes and cubic-substances, into the colours, bright or drab, garish or dingy, that surround us, into the very bodies and faces of the people who surround us, into the atmosphere that overhangs it all, into the opaque body of the earth that underprops it all, and, on, on, through these, and beyond these, into the receding hollowness and unthinkable emptiness of interstellar space!

But our own plunge into the cosmos must not stop here. Arrived at the ultimate black gulf between the stellar systems we will suddenly find ourself at the mental limit of that *false infinity*, that mathematical infinity composed of circles of boundlessness, which is the circumference and the

No-Man's-Land of our particular life-dimension. Here we have reached the very Viper's throat of the *rational insanity* that is at the heart of our futility-torment.

You are now at the boundary of human thought, at the point where human consciousness cannot go further *without cracking*. You have reached this point without a movement of your body. You have reached it through all obstacles, through the walls that shut you in if you are indoors, through the air that surrounds you if you are out of doors.

And now what do you find? You find that there is something in your mind, some integral portion of your mind, some innermost background of your mind, that remains—since it has the power of envisaging this ultimate barrier of thought—*outside what it envisages*. This rational thought-barrier is the cause of your feeling of futility; it is itself this futility. It is the futility in you, in Nature, in life. It is the grand Antagonist in the drama of your struggle to be yourself. But you have now discovered by making this thought-voyage from centre to circumference, that both centre *and* circumference are included in your own mind. You are in the system of things but you also are outside the system of things. By plunging to the limit into the ultimate futility you have come out on the other side. The futility that paralysed you has turned out to be an inevitable recoil of your reason when concentrated upon life; but you have become aware, by facing things to the uttermost, that this recoil itself has taken place *within* yourself and therefore does not represent the whole of yourself. It is your logical power, that terrible and insane instrument of your mind, evolved to measure futility and working with the paradoxes of futility, that has betrayed you.

When a human mind thus turns at bay against a universe which it condemns as futile, and against a self which condemns itself as futile, it has only to carry this revolt far enough, till it strikes the ultimate barrier, to know that by its mere *recognition of that barrier* it is already outside it.

A mind that was entirely futile, in a universe entirely futile, would be unable to recognise futility. Real futility would be unconscious of futility. It is because we are *not* this thing that this thing drives us to despair!

It is not our struggle to be happy that is mistaken; it is our false idea that we can find happiness anywhere but in ourselves.

Pleasure can come and go at random and by chance, for it depends on outward things; but happiness does not depend on outward things. It is born of the mind, it is nourished by the mind, it is what rises, like breath in a frosty air, from the mind's wrestling with its fate. We are not born to be happy.

We are born to struggle for happiness. We are born because of pleasure, but we are born in pain. We are surrounded by pain, and we are lucky if our end is painless. But deep within us is a sacred fount, from whose channel, by a resolute habit of the will, we can clear away the litter that obstructs the water of life. Not in what we possess, not in what we achieve, not in the opinion of others, not in hope, not in admiration, not in love, not in anything below or above the sun, is the secret of happiness to be found. It is only to be found in ourselves.

The essential nature of it who can tell? Some possess it whose lives appear as one long tragedy to others; and many lack it who have in appearance everything to bring it into being.

There are those whose lives are full of moments of distracting pleasure who have never been and never will be happy.

And there are failures, derelicts, fools, abjects, idiots, simpletons, paupers, weaklings, dolts, from whose souls, do what Society can, do what the Universe can, there flows, in spite of everything, this undefiled and undefeated spring!

It is a great mystery; but of this we may be sure; there is none born of woman without the fountain-source of this divine element in his being. The only question is, is our will directed resolutely to its evocation or is it not?

We can all love, we can all hate, we can all possess, we can all pity ourselves, we can all condemn ourselves, we can all admire ourselves, we can all be selfish, we can all be unselfish. But below these things there is *something else*. There is a deep, strange, unaccountable response within us to the mystery of life and the mystery of death; and this response subsists below grief and pain and misery and disappointment, below all care and all futility.

And the startling thing about this response is, that it is independent of love, independent of pleasure, independent of hope, and can continue, as long as we remain ourselves, in spite of all reason, to the end of our days.

JOHN COWPER POWYS

JOHN COWPER POWYS was born on October 8, 1872, in Derbyshire, England, the eldest of eleven children, all but one of whom are still living. Among them are Theodore and Llewelyn, both writers of distinction, and Philippa, a poetess. His father, the Vicar of Shirley, was descended from the ancient princes of Mid-Wales, and his mother sprang from a line that included the poets William Cowper and John Donne. After graduation from Corpus Christi College, Cambridge, Mr. Powys began a series of novels, including DUCDAME and WOOD AND STONE, and embarked upon his extraordinary career as essayist, poet, philosopher and lecturer. For years he lectured through every county of England and every state of America, winning to himself devoted adherents and more ferocious enemies than probably any other speaker can claim. A few years ago Mr. Powys abandoned the lecture platform and urban life in general and moved to a small farm in Columbia County, New York, the scenery of which particularly delighted him because of its marked resemblance to his native Derbyshire. Save for semi-annual excursions to the city for a hair-cut by his favorite barber, Mr. Powys remained in utter seclusion on his farm. His aim in all this, he explained, was "the attainment of a certain kind of happiness by means of the simplification of life. Earning my living by my pen, I am rendered independent of both flattery of and subservience to others. I have simplified my diet until I live on nothing but bread and butter, eggs, tea and honey. I have simplified my reading until I read nothing except Homer and the old English novelists. I am accepted by my neighbors as something of a freak, but the natural good nature and humor of their Dutch blood leads them to be merely indulgent to the crazy vagaries of an Englishman." In the summer of 1934, after an absence of twenty years, Mr. Powys returned to England. He is pleasantly ensconced in a thatched cottage in Dorsetshire and plans to remain there permanently.